COMMUNIO SANCTORUM

The Church as the Communion of Saints

Bilateral Working Group of
the German National Bishops'
Conference and the Church Leadership
of the United Evangelical
Lutheran Church of Germany

Translated by
Mark W. Jeske, Michael Root,
and Daniel R. Smith

LITURGICAL PRESS

Collegeville, Minnesota

www.litpress.org

A title of the Unitas Books series published by the Liturgical Press

Other titles available in the Unitas Books series:

Justification and the Future of the Ecumenical Movement: The Joint Declaration on the Doctrine of Justification
  William G. Rusch, ed.

I Believe, Despite Everything: Reflections of an Ecumenist
  Jean-Marie R. Tillard

Visible Church—Visible Unity: Ecumenical Ecclesiology and "The Great Tradition of the Church"
  Ola Tjørhom

1	2	3	4	5	6	7	8

Library of Congress Cataloging-in-Publication Data

Communio Sanctorum. English.
    Communio Sanctorum : the church as the communion of saints / Bilateral Working Group of the German National Bishops' Conference and the Church Leadership of the United Evangelical Lutheran Church of Germany ; translated by Mark W. Jeske, Michael Root, and Daniel R. Smith.
        p.   cm. — (Unitas books)
    Includes bibliographical references.
    ISBN 0-8146-2566-5 (pbk. : alk. paper)
    1. Lutheran Church—Relations—Catholic Church.   2. Catholic Church—Relations—Lutheran Church.   3. Communion of saints.   I. Bilaterale Arbeitsgruppe der Deutschen Bischofskonferenz und der Kirchenleitung der Vereinigten Evangelisch-Lutherischen Kirche Deutschlands.   II. Title.   III. Series.

BX8063.7.C3C6613 2005
262'.73—dc22

2004007837

Unitas Books

On the eve of his crucifixion, Jesus prayed that his followers "may all be one" (John 17:21). Christians believe that this promise is fulfilled in the church. The church is Christ's body, and his body cannot be divided. And yet, the churches today live in contradiction to that promise. Churches that recognize in another Christian community an embodiment of the one church of Jesus Christ still too often find that they cannot live in true communion with them. This contradiction between the church's unity and its division has driven the ecumenical movement over the last century.

The pursuit of unity will require more than a few mutual adjustments among the churches. Ecumenism must involve true conversion, a conversion both of hearts and minds, of the will and the intellect. We all must learn to think in new ways about the teachings and practices of the church. Division has become deeply embedded in the everyday life and thought of the churches. Thinking beyond division will require a new outlook.

Unitas Books seeks to serve the rethinking that is a necessary part of the ecumenical movement. Some books in the series will directly address important topics of ecumenical discussion; others will chart and analyze the ecumenical movement itself. All will be concerned with the church's unity. Their authors will be ecumenical experts from a variety of Christian traditions, but the books will be written for a wider audience of interested clergy and laypersons. We hope they will be informative for the expert and the newcomer alike.

The unity we seek will be a gift of the Holy Spirit. The Spirit works through means, however, and one of the Spirit's means is careful theological reflection and articulate communication. We hope that this series may be used by the Spirit so that the unity won by Christ may be more fully visible "so that the world may believe" (John 17:21).

Norman A. Hjelm
Michael Root
William G. Rusch

The series editor responsible for this volume is Michael Root.

Contents

Foreword by the Chairs

With a mandate from the German Bishops' Conference and the leadership of the United Evangelical Lutheran Church of Germany (VELKD), the second Bilateral Working Group dealt with the subject *Communio Sanctorum: The Church as the Communion of Saints.* The Working Group now submits the results of this dialogue in order begin a discussion of the questions addressed that will reveal the tenability of the positions suggested or lead to other clarifications that could be accepted by the participating churches.

This text continues the dialogue between our churches that began with the commissioning of a first Bilateral Working Group in 1976 and led to the document *Communion in Word and Sacrament [Kirchengemeinschaft in Wort und Sakrament]* in 1984.[1] After this document had been published with the approval of the German Bishops' Conference and the leadership of the VELKD, both churches began a process of response. The response of the VELKD (1985) and the response of the German Bishops' Conference (1987) were published together in 1988.[2]

As a result of the study *Communion in Word and Sacrament,* the leadership of the VELKD declared that the Reformation's condemnations of the Mass as an "abomination" and the pope as "Antichrist" do not apply to the present teaching of the Catholic Church nor to practices oriented to that teaching. This conclusion has already found expression in the edition of the Lutheran Confessions for the parish[3] and was confirmed by the 1994 response of the VELKD to the document *The Condemnations of the Reformation Era: Do They Still Divide?*[4]

In connection with the process of reception in both churches, an official meeting took place on October 1, 1986 in Hanover between the representatives of the German Bishops' Conference and the Bishops'

Conference of the VELKD. There it was decided to continue the dialogue and to constitute a new Bilateral Working Group. This second Working Group convened in 1987 with the mandate to address the open questions raised in the responses of both sides and to further clarify questions about the essence of the church as well as its offices, including that of the papacy. Finally, the hitherto bracketed issues concerning canon law and the veneration of Mary and the saints were to be discussed.

The theme *"Communio Sanctorum"* proved to be a suitable framework for treating the ecclesiological issues. We asked accordingly how statements of each particular doctrinal tradition could be brought into a positive relationship with the positions of the partner. We were able to establish commonalities that not only confirmed the content of *Communion in Word and Sacrament* but also went beyond it. In the process, it also became clear that we are accustomed to approaching many topics in differing ways. To what extent this involves conflicting viewpoints is still not completely clear.

In this study, the Working Group entered into new territory, especially concerning the following issues:

- the interaction of the witnessing authorities[5] in the discovery and proclamation of the truth of the gospel: Holy Scripture, tradition, the believers' sense of the faith (or the priesthood of all believers), the magisterium, theology;

- the role of a ministry to the unity of the church on a universal level and the related questions of the papal office;

- the community of the saints beyond death (eschatology; prayer for the dead; invocation of the saints; Mary, the mother of the Lord).

What the Working Group presents on its theme represents a particular state of the discussion. It provides a basis for asking in the churches whether and where common approaches to clarifying the issues are possible. The Working Group was aware that many of the approaches considered still face great obstacles. Paragraph 198 may appear to many as an indication of the problems involved in an agreement on papal infallibility and a papal primacy of jurisdiction since it is not clear at present how clarification and practical application could be achieved. Nevertheless, the Working Group did not wish to drop the subject despite various reservations of individual members; it wanted to take up the invitation of Pope John Paul II to join in a dialogue about a contemporary and ecumenically acceptable form of the papal office.

A large number of the questions raised in the two responses to *Communion in Word and Sacrament* could be dealt within the framework of the general theme *"Communio Sanctorum":*

- the doctrine of Holy Scripture (IV.1);

- the concept and number of the sacraments (IV.2);

- the relationship between the priesthood of all believers and ecclesiastical office (VI.1).

Other questions from the responses to *Communion in Word and Sacrament*—for example, the relationship between the visibility and hiddeness of the church, its holiness and sinfulness, as well as the position of canon law—were taken up in the setting of the international dialogue and were therefore not additionally dealt with by the Working Group. When the results from the international dialogue are referred to here, that does not mean that these have already been received by the churches. Rather, this shows how the dialogues at different levels overlap and mutually enrich each other.

The Working Group proceeded methodologically according to the new principles of ecumenical hermeneutics. Basic for these principles is the recognition that the unity sought does not imply uniformity but a diversity in which remaining differences do not become a church-dividing force. Correspondingly the goal of the dialogue is not a consensus in the sense of a complete identity of opinion but a "differentiated consensus," which contains two different statements:

- the agreement reached in the fundamental and essential content of a hitherto controversial doctrine;

- an explanation how and why the remaining doctrinal differences can be accepted without undercutting the basis and essence of the agreement.

The method of "differentiated consensus" was followed already in the study *The Condemnations of the Reformation Era: Do They Still Divide?* It requires two steps:

First, one must test whether the doctrines of one side really exclude the authentic concern of the other. If not, one must then ask whether the concerns and main points of interpretation that are urgent for the doctrine of one side are clearly enough preserved in the doctrine of the other that they cannot be overlooked or misunderstood.[6]

This method, borne by the growing familiarity and experienced community in belief, has shown itself to be helpful in our dialogue.

On the basis of its appointment by respective churches, the Bilateral Working Group understands itself as a national counterpart to the international Roman Catholic-Lutheran Joint Commission. It presents the document *Communio Sanctorum* as a contribution to the dialogue between our churches on both the national and international levels. In the text the statements of other dialogues are taken up, reaffirmed, expanded, and extended. The Working Group especially welcomed impulses from the following documents:

- *The Condemnations of the Reformation Era: Do They Still Divide?* (Protestant-Catholic dialogue in Germany) and the responses to it;

- *Church and Justification* (international Roman Catholic-Lutheran Joint Commission)

- *Joint Declaration on the Doctrine of Justification* (Lutheran World Federation-Roman Catholic Church)

The bilateral Working Group requests the sponsoring churches to examine how far they can make their own the assertions attained in this document. At the same time it invites members of the theological faculties to participate critically in the discussion, to examine the approaches presented, and to contribute to the continuing clarifications.

Würzburg-Weissenhaus, January 25, 2000

Paul-Werner Scheele   Ulrich Wilckens
Bishop of Würzburg   Bishop emeritus of Lübeck

Notes

[1] *Kirchengemeinschaft in Wort und Sakrament* (Paderborn: Bonifatius, 1984; hereafter referred to as KWS).

[2] Published in *Texte aus der VELKD*, no. 36; *Arbeitshilfen der Deutschen Bischofskonferenz*, no. 59.

[3] *Unser Glaube: Die Bekenntnisschriften der evangelisch-lutherischen Kirche. Ausgabe für die Gemeinde* (Gütersloh, 1991) 451f., 466, 515f., 520.

[4] *Texts from the VELKD*, no. 42 (1996); see also *Lehrverurteilungen im Gespräch* (Göttingen: Vandenhoeck & Ruprecht, 1993) 57–160 (hereafter referred to as LVIG).

[5] [Trans.: The Working Group uses its own term, *Bezeugungsinstanz*, here translated rather literally as "witnessing authority." The wording carries the implication that the various authorities referred to are themselves witnesses to something else, to God and the gospel.]

[6] Compare *The Condemnations of the Reformation Era: Do They Still Divide?* Karl Lehmann and Wolfhart Pannenberg, eds. (Minneapolis: Fortress Press, 1990) 40, 15–19.

A Catholic Preface by George H. Tavard

Whatever happens in the church takes place in a cultural context that varies constantly since it is affected by all sorts of historical events. And these events are themselves situated in a broad spiritual horizon that one may call divine providence, the will or purpose of God, the abiding presence of Christ, the creative power of the Spirit . . . .

The persons who are baptized, and who believe the promises of God extended to us in Jesus Christ, thus belong, not only to their province or tribe or nation, but also, and first of all, to a community that is defined by faith and baptism. This, community, also called church or communion *(koinonia)*, is both visible and invisible. And, in spite of cultural and individual differences among its members, it is one.

In this horizon Catholics see the role of the bishop of Rome: to show a solicitude for all the churches, on the model of, and in succession to, the apostle Peter, who was called to feed the flock of Christ and to strengthen his brothers. The history of the church and of the papacy, however, is replete with disasters. Pope Paul VI paradoxically pointed to one of them when he declared, in 1967, "The pope, as we all know, is undoubtedly the gravest obstacle in the path of ecumenism."

Certainly this statement was by no means an infallible proclamation. It was, nevertheless, simply true. The Reformation had its occasion in the actions of Leo X, who tolerated the sale of indulgences and excommunicated Martin Luther. The divisions among Christians was made worse when Pius V excommunicated Queen Elizabeth. They were widened when Pius IX solemnly defined the Immaculate Conception of Mary and papal infallibility. In 1950 the definition of Mary's Assumption by Pius XII added another obstacle to Christian reunion.

In spite of all this, the Catholic church was launched on the path of ecumenism by Vatican Council II and the two popes who presided over it, John XXIII and Paul VI. As it is engaged in this movement, of which John Paul II wrote in the encyclical *Ut unum sint* that it is irreversible, the Catholic church is now facing the dilemma that the communion of saints exists in a situation of division.

Catholic and Lutheran theologians in Germany have boldly confronted the ensuing questions in the joint statement that is now presented to English-speaking readers. Catholics should pay close attention to this text, for it is only in our communion together as Christians that the disunity we have inherited can be overcome.

A Lutheran Preface by John Reumann

This bilateral statement on a phrase in the Apostles' Creed, "I believe in . . . the communion of saints . . . ," speaks far beyond German Roman Catholics and Lutherans, for it is oriented toward "a structural form of unity" for "world Christianity" (#273). Through the "useful framework" of *communio sanctorum*, it incorporates treatment of Christian saints in church and world (6.1) and beyond death (7.1) and a *communio* ecclesiology (chap. 3; ##143–52), with attention to the word of God, sacraments, justification, the papacy, and life in the churches today. The Working Group worked in such a way as to spell out historic impasses, what each communion can now say, and what they can say together; e.g., (82)–(84) on sacraments and their number (no, "sacrament" and "act of blessing" is not a formulation with same-sex unions in mind).

The result of thirteen years of work, the document exhibits the theological and biblical thoroughness one expects from Lutherans and Catholics in Germany, without overwhelming us with footnotes. The treatment of the significance of Justification by Faith also shows a fine concern for societal setting (119)–(122) in the "public arena," "fabric of society," and public witness. A predecessor statement on *Communion in Word and Sacrament* (1976–84) has never been translated. The way, however, it received official response by the German churches and practical application (e.g., in texts for lay people) bodes well for achieving "differentiated consensus" on items in *Communio Sanctorum* (see the Foreword by the Chairs). On a problem with "great obstacles," papal infallibility and jurisdiction according to Vatican I, #(198) pinpoints lines on which "an official interpretation" of highest authority would be welcome.

The study draws especially on three documents, all available in English: *The Condemnations of the Reformation Era,* one of several volumes by a Catholic-Lutheran/Reformed/Union Church Working Group, 1981–85 (Foreword by the Chairs, n. 6); the 1994 volume from the international Lutheran-Roman Catholic Joint Commission, *Church and Justification: Understanding the Church in the Light of the Doctrine of Justification* (Geneva: LWF); and the 1999 *Joint Declaration on the Doctrine of Justification* (Grand Rapids: Eerdmans, 2000), a platform for future work which other communions may make their own. Surprisingly, Faith and Order Paper no. 166, *On the Way to Fuller Koinonia* (Geneva: WCC, 1994) is not cited. Nor, for that matter, *The Church as Communion: Lutheran Contributions to Ecclesiology,* LWF Documentation 42 (Geneva 1997), more substantial than the 1990 Strasbourg Institute paper (chap. 3, n. 3).

Readers will observe that American dialogue is hailed for exegetical work in #(183) n. 66, presumably *Peter in the New Testament: A Collaborative Assessment by Protestant and Roman Catholic Scholars* (Minneapolis: Augsburg/New York: Paulist, 1973; repr. Eugene, Or.: Wipf and Stock, 2002; German tr., *Der Petrus der Bibel* [Stuttgart: Calwer Verlag/Katholisches Bibelwerk, 1976), but not *Papal Primacy and the Universal Church,* Lutherans and Catholics in Dialogue V (Minneapolis: Augsburg, 1973). They will read with surprise, "Mary has previously scarcely been subject of ecumenical dialogue" (258) and may want to compare *The One Mediator, the Saints and Mary,* LCID VIII (Minneapolis: Augsburg, 1992), which is also pertinent to chap. 7. But chap. 4, 1.1-8, on "instances" where witness becomes definitive, treats overall aspects not found in *Scripture and Tradition,* Lutherans and Catholics in Dialogue IX (Minneapolis: Augsburg, 1995). On the church, local, regional, and universal (148), cf. the forthcoming *The Church as Koinonia of Salvation,* Lutherans and Catholics in Dialogue X.

One may decide, on an initial reading, my (church's) view cannot entertain what is said in *Communio Sanctorum* about this point or that. But "reception" involves longer consideration of how, reciprocally, we can work from the data and insights here toward comprehensive agreement (*magnum consensus,* #58) of the faithful. Such is its mission.

John Reumann
Ministerium of Pennsylvania Professor, emeritus
Lutheran Theological Seminary at Philadelphia

Introduction

Ecumenical steps in Germany are understood as one aspect of the worldwide ecumenical pursuit of Christian unity. The dialogues between the regional Lutheran churches in Germany and the Roman Catholic Church began with this in mind in the mid-1970s. From the beginning, the Bilateral Working Group initiated by the United Evangelical-Lutheran Church of Germany (VELKD) and the German Bishops' Conference understood itself as a regional corollary of the Lutheran-Roman Catholic International Commission mandated by the Lutheran World Federation and the Pontifical Council for Promoting Christian Unity. The Working Group's intention has been to make its own contribution for the support and development of international Lutheran-Catholic efforts. To this end, a responsible and critical dialogue needed to be pursued.

The institution of the Bilateral Working Group had to take into consideration the particular confessional relations that exist in Germany. The legal recognition of the Reformation in the Holy Roman Empire came through its connection with state authority. As a result, the Lutheran churches in Germany developed as regional state churches under the direction of the regional prince as overseer or *summepiskopus*. After this rule of the church by the princes collapsed with the end of the German Empire in 1918, the regional churches developed their own constitutions and from the beginning sought associations with other such churches on the basis of their respective Reformation confessions. After the Second World War, the United Evangelical-Lutheran Church of Germany was founded to overcome the splintering of the regional churches, but not all the Lutheran churches were won for this plan. Some churches with a Lutheran character saw themselves as Union churches with a differing set of connections. Thus, the Evangelical Church in Germany

(EKD), as a federation that included Lutheran and non-Lutheran regional churches, came over time to have an increasing significance. Ecumenical dialogues between the Catholic church and the VELKD have remained embedded in these specific German Protestant relationships, as was already the case with the Ecumenical Study Group of Catholic and Protestant theologians established in 1946 (the so-called Jaeger-Stählin Group, named for its two first presidents), in which the majority of the Protestant theologians were Lutheran.

In view of this complex ecumenical situation, it was surprising that the Bilateral Working Group created in 1976 was able to present a significant result by 1984. A clear agreement on the goal of ecumenical dialogue was blocked by the still extensively unclarified and controversial topic of ecclesiology. The intention of the Working Group was to make a contribution toward a clarification in this area. *Communion in Word and Sacrament [Kirchengemeinschaft in Wort und Sakrament]* wished to be a stock-taking along the way, an appropriation and testing of the results so far achieved, in order to stimulate their reception in the churches involved. If it is clear that the goal of all ecumenical agreement can only be "full communion," then the goal is not the absorption of one church by the other, but mutual recognition on the basis of the common faith, communion in the sacraments, and communion in apostolic ministry. On the way to this goal, we need to clarify what Lutherans and Catholics mean when they use the word "church." Significant differences exist in the traditions of both churches in the understanding of the precise relation between the church's visible institutional form and its hidden essence, grasped only by faith. This problem comes to a head in the question of what in detail is constitutive for the church's visible communion. Through a step-by-step definition of the problem, the dialogue succeeded in marking the areas constitutive for church fellowship. "Communion in Word and Sacrament is also communion in ministerial office." There is only one office in the church, to which is entrusted the preaching of the word of God and the administration of the sacraments. Significant differences continue to exist in the question of stages within this office.

Both the Catholic German Bishops' Conference and the Bishops' Conference and Church Council of the VELKD made official responses to the document, which were published together. The Catholic church appreciated the inclusion of the fundamental sacramental dimension of the church as well as the presentation of an ecclesiology of communion. The Church Council of the VELKD declared that the Reformation condemnations of the Mass as an "abomination" and of the pope as "Antichrist" do not apply to the present teaching of the Catholic Church. Both churches were of the conviction that a fundamental agreement existed in the understanding of the church so that talk of a "fundamental difference" or "fundamental disagreement" was not possible. Nevertheless, important differences obviously continued to exist.

As important as the achieved progress was, both sides viewed further dialogue as needed. The intention was not a change of perspective in the dialogue but a deepening of the question. The theme of the communion of the saints proved to be an appropriate framework for addressing the ecclesiological questions. The concern was not simply to seek further consensus in ecclesiology but also to test whether common approaches to clarifying outstanding problems could be found. *Communio Sanctorum* thus is to be understood as a statement of the issues. In this regard, this new Catholic-Lutheran document is a true step forward in two respects. First, it applies the new principles of ecumenical hermeneutics, in the sense of the method of a "differentiated consensus" as used in the *Joint Declaration on the Doctrine of Justification* of 1999. Second, it takes up topics of considerable difficulty, e.g., teaching authority, papacy, and a petrine ministry within the communion of the church. Precisely by taking up newer hermeneutical methods, *Communion Sanctorum* brings to light new paths toward the solution of problems formerly considered insoluble. Here lies the significance of this document beyond the German context.

Prof. Dr. Wolfgang Thönissen
Paderborn, Germany
March 22, 2004

Chapter 1

The Communion of Saints According to the Confession of the Church

---

(1) In the New Testament, believers are called "saints" (1 Cor 1:2; 2 Cor 1:1; Eph 4:12; Col 1:12). The church is therefore the communion[1] or gathering of saints. In this confession, our churches are in agreement. The document *Communion in Word and Sacrament* declares: The church is communion *through* Jesus Christ, *with* Jesus Christ, and *in* Jesus Christ. This "communion through, with, and in Jesus Christ is communion in the Holy Spirit."[2]

(2) "I believe in the communion of saints." With this statement from the Apostles' Creed we confess that the Holy Spirit is the life-giving principle of the one holy church. The Apostles' Creed has its origin in the liturgy of baptism of the early western church. In the course of preparation, individual candidates for baptism "received" these words; before the administration of the sacrament they were required in the presence of the congregation to "give them back," i.e., to declare as their own the content the words express. They thereby explicitly confessed and announced their own unsubstitutible faith: "I believe." Thus their individual faith presented itself as identical with the faith of the whole church.

This points already to the fundamental relationship of the individual to the community and vice versa: *I* am always able to believe only because there is a *we*, a community of believers, in which I received the faith; the faith of the *community*, however, is sustained by the faith of the

1

many *individuals,* who were called by God into community.[3] Faith and community belong together in the most intimate sense.

(3) The faith of the individual and of the community has various dimensions. The core of the Christian faith is faith in God, the complete and unconditional trust merited only by the Triune God. Because God "spoke to our ancestors in many and various ways by the prophets, but in these last days he has spoken to us by a Son" (Heb 1:1f.), this faith has a content. God revealed himself in that he said and did something. Whoever believes in God therefore also believes something, namely, the revelation of God in word and deed.

(4) The "communion of saints" is such a content of the faith. According to the Apostles Creed, this communion arises as the life-giving principle of the church from faith in the Holy Spirit. The expression "communion of saints" is first found in a baptismal creed from the end of the fourth century.[4] It relates first to the holy gifts that God gives to the church, especially in the Eucharist. Only on the basis of this comprehensively foundational gift do those who receive it become "saints": the participation *(koinonia, communio)* in the holy gifts *(sancta)* founds the communion *(koinonia, communio)* of sanctified Christians *(sancti)* with Christ and among each other. This happens in the Holy Spirit, who is the gift of the Risen One.

(5) Because the communion of saints is communion with the Risen One, it transcends all boundaries and limitations of time and space.
     Niceta of Remesiana (†414), the earliest witness for the expression "communion of saints," writes:
     "The church is simply the community *(congregatio)* of all the saints. All who from the beginning of the world were or are or will be justified—whether Patriarchs, like Abraham, Isaac and Jacob, or Prophets, whether Apostles or martyrs, or any others—make up one church, because they are made holy by one faith and way of life, stamped with one Spirit, made into one body whose head, as we are told, is Christ. I go further. The angels and virtues and powers in heaven are co-members in this one church, for, as the Apostle teaches us, in Christ 'all things whether on the earth or in the heavens, have been reconciled' (Col 1:20). You must believe, therefore, that in this one church you are gathered into the *communion of saints [communionem sanctorum].* You must know that this is the one Catholic Church established

throughout the world, and with it you must remain in unshaken communion *[communionem]*."[5]

According to Niceta, whoever is "just" belongs to the communion of saints. This communion stands in the midst of the world and at the same time transcends those boundaries "upward." In service to the world, it is to give witness that this transcendence is oriented towards God.

(6) "I believe in the communion of the saints." This confession expresses a firm trust that the church does not thank itself for its being and work but that it has its place in the creative and redemptive work of the triune God. Therefore the church in its innermost nature is a mystery *(mysterium)*. It exists in history. Thus, it participates in history's visible and also sinful structures, but it is not absorbed by them. It receives its life from the word of God and the sacraments. At the same time, it also experiences its limitations: its knowledge is only in part (1 Cor 13:9), and its life from God's gifts is threatened through human weakness and sin. These limitations apply also to the form of the church, its ministries and offices.

(7) A series of issues for dialogue between our churches result from the tension between the mystery of the church and its form in the world. Many questions have already been clarified in earlier dialogues, e.g., questions related to ministerial office, also the office of the bishop.[6] We enter new territory with regard to the following topics:

- the interaction of varying witnessing authorities in the discovery and proclamation of the revealed truth (Holy Scripture, tradition, the believers' sense of the faith, the church's magisterium, theology);

- the role of a ministry to the unity of the universal church ("the Petrine Ministry");

- the communion of saints beyond death (eschatology; prayer for the dead; veneration of the saints; Mary, the mother of the Lord).

The confession of the communion of saints has proven to be a useful framework for addressing these topics. On certain topics, it seemed necessary to offer biblical and historical arguments. It was also possible to adopt or refer to already existing dialogue results and thus contribute to their reception.

Notes

[1] [Trans.: The German term *Gemeinschaft* can be translated as "communion," "community," or "fellowship." It is generally translated here as "communion" to catch the sense of communion in and with Christ and the Spirit that is theologically fundamental in this context.]

[2] KWS, pars. 2–5.

[3] Among other ways, this close relationship is shown in the liturgical use of the shared early Christian creeds in which one (the Apostles' Creed) begins with "I believe," while the other (Nicene Creed) begins with "We believe." The Apostles' Creed is a confession for baptism: here the acceptance of faith by the individual is decisive. As a conciliar confession, the Nicene Creed is a doctrinal confession: the whole community of believers accepts the creed of the church assembly.

[4] Heinrich Denzinger, *Enchiridion symbolorum definitionum et declarationum de rebus fidei et morum,* 37th ed., Peter Hünermann, ed. (Freiburg i.B.: Herder, 1991; hereafter DH), par. 19.

[5] Niceta of Remesiana, "Explanation of the Creed," in *The Fathers of the Church: A New Translation,* vol. 7, R. J. Deferrari, ed., Gerald G. Walsh, trans. (New York: Fathers of the Church, Inc., 1949) 49–50.

[6] Roman Catholic-Lutheran Joint Commission, *The Ministry in the Church* (1981), in *Growth in Agreement: Reports and Agreed Statements of Ecumenical Conversations on a World Level,* Harding Meyer and Lukas Vischer, eds. (New York: Paulist Press, 1984) 248–75; KWS, pars. 56–76.

Chapter 2

The Church According to the Witness of Holy Scripture

1. The Calling of the Church

(8) The Holy Scriptures of the Old and New Testaments, in their entirety and in the individual writings, show God's action in human history. God calls Israel to be his people of the covenant, shows them the way, and is present in the midst of his people. In sending Jesus as the Messiah of Israel, God confirms his faithfulness to his people, while at the same time constituting it anew from Jews and Gentiles in the horizon of the eschatological promise of salvation for all peoples. The church understands itself fundamentally on the basis of this salvific action of God.

(9) According to the witness of the New Testament, the "church" is encountered first in the form of the disciples who were called by Jesus and who followed him. Their discipleship joined them together with him in a living communion. This communion makes possible their being sent to proclaim the gospel and heal the sick.

(10) Communion with Jesus Christ and being sent by him also determine the appearance of the post-Easter church. It is founded on the central event of the death and resurrection of Jesus. In baptism, individual Christians receive strength through the Holy Spirit, who enables and moves them to proclaim the gospel to all people and to call them into a new community of God's people comprised of Jews and Gentiles.

(11)   The promise of the "new covenant" (Jer 31:31-34) is thus realized in the church, whose "foundation is Jesus Christ" (1 Cor 3:11). In this age the church already shares in the eschatological treasures of this covenant, but it awaits the fullness of these treasures to be finally revealed with the return of Christ. It has the form of God's people "on the way." With confidence, it moves toward its goal in the fulfillment of its mission.

New Testament texts, in accord with their respective situations and times, witness to the call of the church from different perspectives. Several important accents should be emphasized.

(12)   Central and fundamental in the proclamation and teaching of the *apostle Paul* is the gospel of God's salvific action in Jesus Christ. It calls people to faith, and on its basis they respond as the faithful. As the faithful stand individually as justified sinners before God, so they also become at the same time members of the community of the faithful, the church. Through faith and baptism all become "one in Christ Jesus" (Gal 3:26-28), whoever they may be and from wherever they may come. The local church and the church in its entirety in all localities is the body of Christ, permeated and held together by the one Spirit of God. In its members and in its entirety it becomes the witness of God's power of salvation in the world, the advocate of the "new creation" in the transitory, old world. The Letter to the Colossians and Letter to the Ephesians (Col 1:18-20; 2:19; Eph 4:11-16) strengthen this view of the church as the sign and bearer of divine salvation for the world.

(13)   How much the church is bound up with the fate of its Lord Jesus Christ is shown in the First Letter of Peter. The church in the congregations "in the Dispersion" also as a whole participates in the path of suffering of its Lord. It is capable of this because in confident joy it awaits the completion of salvation. "Do not be surprised at the fiery ordeal that is taking place among you to test you, as though something strange were happening to you. But rejoice insofar as you are sharing Christ's sufferings, so that you may also be glad and shout for joy when his glory is revealed" (1 Pet 4:12f.).

(14)   The *Gospels,* each in its own particular way, bear witness to the church as the circle of disciples called by Jesus. As such the church is constantly oriented towards the message and the work of Jesus whose mission it is to carry on.

(15) *Matthew* presents this forcefully with the word of the resurrected Lord to his disciples: "Go therefore and make disciples of all nations, baptizing them in the name of the Father and of the Son and of the Holy Spirit, and teaching them to obey everything that I have commanded you. And remember, I am with you always, to the end of the age" (Matt 28:19f.). The proclamation of the gospel and the reception of baptism should lead people to a lived discipleship of Jesus, for which especially the Sermon of the Mount provides an authoritative guide. In acting according to the command of Jesus, the disciples, who collectively form the "ekklesia" (Matt 16:18; 18:17), become "the light of the world," "a city built on a hill," and thus a sign for people "so that they may see your good works and give glory to your Father in heaven" (Matt 5:14-16).

(16) *Luke*, above all in The Acts of the Apostles, portrayed the way of the church into the *Oikumene*, that is, into the entire world, as its salvation-historical mission. It takes this path under the impetus of the Holy Spirit, in the confidence worked by the Holy Spirit, and with the testimony that faith in Jesus Christ is the path to salvation revealed by God. "For there is no other name under heaven given among mortals by which we must be saved" (Acts 4:12).

2. The Form of the Church's Life

(17) Determinative for the form of the church is its inner liveliness, worked by the Holy Spirit. It is one and the same Spirit who distributes to individuals his gifts as he wills, so that "all the members of the body, though many, are one body"—in Christ (1 Cor 12:11f.). Its life is shaped by the reception of God's gifts and the praise of God's goodness in worship. The form of the church is thereby determined by worship. The common liturgical thanksgiving of believers in the Eucharist is at work in "everyday worship," in life and service with and for each other, as attested in the life of the early church (Acts 2:42-47). Thus the gospel finds its way into the world through the witness of the life of believers. Worship *(leiturgia)*, service *(diakonia)*, and witness *(martyria)* belong together. In them the liveliness of the church worked by the Holy Spirit is evident.

(18) The *one* Spirit, who enlivens the church and preserves its members in unity, also awakens in it the forces that serve in a *special* way to

build up the individual congregations and the church as a whole. The apostle Paul points to this when he begins his enumeration of the gifts of the Spirit with the special ministries of apostles, prophets, and teachers (1 Cor 12:28). The special gifts given from the Lord to the church serve to equip the saints for the work of their ministry, the building up of the body of Christ (Eph 4:11f.).

(19)   Fundamental for the building up of the church is the office of *apostle*. Because the apostles are called and sent by the Lord himself, they have an exceptional authority. They care for the proclamation of the gospel in word and sacrament and for the congregation which grows from that proclamation. The post-apostolic church remains dependent on the tradition of the apostles. An office of leadership developed that shared in the authority of the apostles and cared for the appropriate transmission of the apostolic tradition. In its constant reference to the apostles, this office is itself *apostolic*. The apostolic office serves the continuity and identity of the church, and thus its unity.

3. The Primitive Church:
Image and Impulse for the Church in Its Further History

(20)   According to the depiction in the Acts of the Apostles, the church of early Christianity is a *faith witness* for the world and an *example* for the church on its further path. "They devoted themselves to the apostles' teaching and fellowship, to the breaking of bread and the prayers" (Acts 2:42). In these words the fundamental experience of the early church finds expression.

(21)   From its historical beginnings on, the essential elements of the church's calling are given to it, making it unmistakable in the world and distinct from every other community. The church guards this, its own originally given form of life, in constant practice of the discipleship of Jesus, in the "testing" and "discernment of the spirits" (1 Thess 5:21; 1 Cor 12:10; 1 John 4:1), and in trust in the work of the Holy Spirit which "reminds you of all that I said to you" (John 14:26). From this fundamental spiritual orientation, the church gains the powers of renewal in all its members and also the necessary openness for further historical developments and challenges.

4. Communion with the Angels and Saints

(22)   According to the understanding of the New Testament, the church not only encompasses the congregation of believers on earth, but also the great invisible congregations of angels and saints already glorified. It knows itself to be called together with the "great multitude . . . from every nation, from all tribes and peoples and languages" and with "all the angels" who sing of the "salvation" coming from God and give him alone the worship he deserves (Rev 7:9-12).

The knowledge of this encompassing community of saints (cf. Heb 12:22-24) strengthens and inspires the community of believers on earth in the engagement with which it faces the pressing, social challenges of its time. On its earthly pilgrimage it already celebrates the salvation that it awaits from God and that it will attain as the encompassing "communion of saints" at the end of the ages.

Chapter 3

The Communion of Saints in the Love of the Triune God

---

1. The Church as Communio

(23) The Gospel of John witnesses that all who belong to Jesus are included in the intimate communion between the Father and the Son: ". . . that they may all be one. As you, Father are in me and I am in you, may they also be in us" (John 17:21). The most intimate union of believers with God consists accordingly in their participation in that intimate communion of love that exists in God himself between the Father and the Son and a share in which the Spirit of God gives to the church. The unity of the church "is a mystery that finds its highest exemplar and principle in the unity of the persons of the Trinity: the unity of the one God, the Father and the Son in the Holy Spirit."[1] This holds for the communion of individuals within the local congregation and for the communion of congregations in the universal church.

(24) Such notions of a "*communio*-ecclesiology" that had been developed in the early church are characteristic today in the teachings of the Orthodox as well as the Roman Catholic[2] churches, the Anglican as well as the Lutheran churches,[3] and are significant shaping factors in the dialogues between them.[4]

(25) In the New Testament, the foundation, meaning, and goal of the church as communion of saints are developed in a multitude of metaphors. Three of these metaphors are to be emphasized; they especially

10

point to the grounding of the communion of saints in the love of the Triune God.

2. The Church as the Wandering People of God

(26)   The church of the New Testament claims for itself Israel's name of honor, "people of God" (cf. 1 Pet 2:9f.). Thereby is expressed simultaneously both the salvation-historical continuity of the church with Israel as well as the breaking in of a new phase of salvation-history in which faith in the one God is concentrated on faith in Jesus Christ, while the community of God's chosen is extended to believers from all nations. In the framework of this dialogue, the question of the precise relation between Israel and the church was not fully explored, but this can be said: on the one hand, an original unity of the church with Israel and Israel with the church is given in the name "people of God"; on the other hand, the nations (Gentiles) are no longer strangers and aliens but citizens with the saints and members of the household of God (Eph 2:19). Jesus, the Messiah, "makes peace and reconciles both to God in one body through the cross" (Eph 2:15f.). So the church as communion of Jews and Gentiles is the new people of God.

(27)   This communion is charged with the proclamation of the gospel, which addresses all persons, women and men of all races and social strata, and calls them together to one people (Rom 1:16). Thus the church is in its mission a proleptic representation and sign of the promised unity of humanity (Rev 5:9f.).

(28)   Just as the way of the people Israel led forty years through the wilderness before they could enter the promised land, so the church as the new people of God pursues a pilgrimage through earthly time, following Christ, who has gone before and leads (Heb 3:15; 5:31; 6:20; 12:2), until at the end of the ages it will enter the rest, peace, and joy of God's kingdom. In his service, God's own people struggle against the God-opposing powers and principalities with the weapons of the Spirit, given them by the Lord (Eph 6:10-16). With a watchful spirit, they stand by one another in ceaseless prayer.

3. The Church as the Body of Christ and the Bride of Christ

(29)   Because Christ died and was raised for his own, he lives in them and they live in him. So through baptism they are not only all together

"one body in Christ, and individually . . . members of one another" (Rom 12:5), but in its entirety the church is *"the* body of Christ" and they are "individually members of it" (1 Cor 12:27). As the various members of the human body work together, so should the members of the body of Christ live together through the gifts of grace, working together and sharing with one another every joy and every suffering (1 Cor 12:14-27; Rom 12:4f.).

(30)   The communion of the Lord with his church is a communion in love: Christ made the church his bride; he gave himself up for her to glorify and sanctify her (Eph 5:25-32). As she is his bride, he will take her to himself forever (Rev 19:7; 21:2, 9; 22:17). Therefore, as long as she is on her earthly pilgrimage, she yearns for her heavenly bridegroom and sets her mind on him (Col 3:1-4).

(31)   The attestations of the church as the body and bride of Christ are images that also point to a sacramental reality: Christ gave himself, his own body, for us and gives us in the Eucharist his body as spiritual food: "Take, eat; this is my body" (Matt 26:26). By sharing in his body (1 Cor 10:16-17), we *are* his body (1 Cor 12:27). Because he alone makes those who belong to him to be members of this body, he is the one head of the body (Col 1:18). In every celebration of the Eucharist, the entire church is present because Christ is present as the head of his body. The whole life of the Christian as a member of his body is a process of growth towards him.

4. The Church as Temple of the Holy Spirit

(32)   In the New Testament the church as a whole is also compared in many ways with a house: It is a "spiritual house" (1 Pet 2:5), "God's building" (1 Cor 3:9), "God's temple" (1 Cor 3:16f; 2 Cor 6:16; Eph 2:21).

(33)   The Spirit is the decisive gift of baptism (John 3:5; Acts 2:38; 2 Cor 1:22, 5:5; Eph 1:13f.; Gal 3:2; Rom 5:5; 1 Thess 4:8; 1 Pet 1:2). Therefore, individual believers may also be called "a temple of the Holy Spirit" (1 Cor 6:19). The *one* Spirit works through the many gifts that the baptized receive as members of the church (1 Cor 12:4-6; Eph 4:4-6). And the gifts of the Spirit are measured by love (1 Cor 13). In that love, the various gifts of the Spirit serve to build up the congregation (1 Cor 8:1, 14:12; Eph 4:16). It is Christ though whom "the whole structure" is held

together and grows into a temple of the Lord, into a dwelling place of God's Spirit (Eph 2:21).

(34)   The foundation is Christ (1 Cor 3:11). He is also the keystone (Eph 2:20). The foundation is laid by the apostles' and prophets' proclamation of the gospel (Eph 2:20). The generations of the church should continue to build upon it. The structure will be complete at the end of the ages. Then the new, heavenly Jerusalem will come down from heaven as "the home of God among mortals" (Rev 21:1-3). In this future city there will be no temple; "for its temple is the Lord God the Almighty and the Lamb" (Rev 21:22). Yet, the city of the living God is present in the here and now when the earthly church in worship participates in the praise offered by those who have been made perfect (Heb 12:22-24).

Notes

[1] Second Vatican Council, Decree on Ecumenism, *Unitatis redintegratio* [UR], 2.

[2] E.g., Second Vatican Council, Dogmatic Constitution on the Church, *Lumen gentium* [LG], 23, 26.

[3] See the study presented in 1990 by the Institute for Ecumenical Research (Strasbourg), *Communio / Koinonia. A New Testament-Early Christian Concept and its Contemporary Appropriation and Significance,* in William G. Rusch, ed., *A Commentary on "Ecumenism: The Vision of the ELCA,"* 119–41 (Minneapolis: Augsburg, 1990).

[4] See, e.g., the document of the 1982 international Roman Catholic-Orthodox dialogue, *The Mystery of the Church and of the Eucharist in the Light of the Mystery of the Holy Trinity:* "Still more radically, because the one and only God is the communion of three persons, the one and only church is a communion of many communities and the local church is a communion of persons. The one and unique church finds her identity in the koinonia of the churches" (III/2), in *Growth in Agreement II:* Reports and Agreed Statements of Ecumenical Conversations on a World Level, 1982–1998, Jeffrey Gros, Harding Meyer, and William G. Rusch, eds. 656f. (Grand Rapids: Eerdmans, 2000). See also the Roman Catholic-Lutheran dialogue, *Facing Unity,* pars. 5–7; KWS, pars. 30, 43, 86–88; as well as *Baptism, Eucharist and Ministry,* pars. B6, E19, E25.

Chapter 4

The Communion of Saints Through
Word and Sacrament

(35) Since God desires community with us humans, he goes to the place where we are to be found: into the world. He is close to us in the midst of our earthly reality. God has become human in Jesus Christ and has made himself subject to the conditions of our life. Accordingly, the Holy Spirit uses earthly, perishable means to give us a place in the communion of God: audible words and visible signs, e.g., water, bread and wine. With this, the Holy Spirit also enters into basic forms of human communication.

(36) In his word, and in the signs that are bound to the word, the sacraments, Christ is present.[1] Through them, he calls people to faith, and effects faith within them. Vatican II says: "They do not only presuppose faith; they also nourish it, strengthen it, and express it, through words and through things."[2] This is reminiscent of the *Augsburg Confession* (CA), article 13: "Concerning the use of sacraments it is taught the sacraments are . . . signs and witnesses of God's will toward us in order thereby to awaken and strengthen our faith. That is why they also require faith and are used rightly when received in faith for the strengthening of faith."[3]

(37) The space in which God encounters human beings through word and sacrament and leads them to faith is the church. In this sense, we can testify together: the church "is the assembly of all believers among

whom the gospel is purely preached and the holy sacraments are administered according to the gospel."[4] The encounter of God with persons through word and sacrament occurs regularly in the worship of the gathered congregation. Since the church lives from the word and the sacraments, it is itself of the word and at the same time sacramentally shaped. The language of Vatican II about the church as "sacrament" has its origin here.[5]

(38)   Word and sacrament are tightly bound to one another: the word of proclamation is audible sign; the sacraments are visible word. In both ways the gospel comes from the outside and bodily touches humans most inwardly, brings them to faith, justifies and sanctifies them, and unites them with God and with one another.

(39)   In the following sections, it will be shown more closely what defines and shapes the church's communion. That which was already stated in the document *Communion in Word and Sacrament* is presupposed. Around the theme of "Communion of Saints" we are dealing:

1. in the section "Word of God," with the finding and proclaiming of the truth in the communion of the church and with the witnessing authorities that work together in this, and

2. in the section "Sacraments," with the meaning of the sacraments for the communion of believers with Christ and one another, and also with the number of sacraments.

1. Word of God

1.1 Revelation and Faith

(40)   Revelation is the self-communication of God in history that has its climax and fulfillment in Jesus Christ, who "by the total reality of his presence and self-manifestation—and by his words and works, his signs and miracles, but above all by his death and glorious resurrection from the dead, crowned through the sending of the Spirit of Truth, completes the work of revelation and confirms it by divine testimony."[6] Through this revelation, God makes his glory known in all the world, so that humans have a share in it, for their salvation: "From his fullness we have all received grace upon grace" (John 1:16).

(41)   The Christian faith has its foundation in the revelation of God in Jesus Christ: the Risen One is present in the midst of his own "to the end of the world" (Matt 28:20). He takes all who believe in him into his service, to testify to him throughout the centuries of history, and ever anew to move persons to the "obedience of faith" (Rom 14:26, cf. Rom 1:5; 2 Cor 10:5-6). "For this faith to be accorded, the prevenient and accompanying grace of God is needed, as well as the interior assistance of the Holy Spirit . . . ."[7] The Holy Spirit brings about the human recognition that this is truly God's word. The fundamental content of faith—God and his saving act in Jesus Christ—has a fundamental shape: the testimony of the first witnesses within the communion of the church. The confession of Jesus Christ—unto martyrdom—awakens new faith.[8]

1.2 The Testimony of Revelation in the Church

(42)   The revelation is delivered through the testifying word. This is experienced as the word of God: it speaks to persons with full power, upon which they can rely totally and without limit. Insofar as those to whom God speaks his word accept this word in faith, salvation is decided on their behalf.[9] Thus it is necessary for persons to recognize the word of God as that which it is, to accept it, and to allow their lives to be determined by it.

(43)   The church lives from the word of God and is at the same time placed in its service. It owes this service to all persons, believers and non-believers alike. It fulfills this inasmuch as it points to the truth of Christ, to Christ as the truth itself. The church has the promise of the Holy Spirit, which leads it in truth: "but the Advocate, the Holy Spirit, that the Father will send in my name, he will teach you everything, and remind you of everything that I have said to you" (John 14:26). The church does have the truth at its disposal. It has the promise that it will remain in the truth if it allows itself constantly to be called back to it.

(44)   Since the church is taken into the service of witnessing to the truth, it speaks with authority—"whether one wants to hear it or not" (2 Tim 4:2). It is thus the addressee of the revelation and at the same time the bearer of its universal mediation. As mediator, the church also stands over against individual believers. It does not derive its authority from itself, however, but rather from the word of God that it proclaims.[10] The church must give itself to the Truth of God in humility

and obedience. It is conscious that its recognition of and testimony to the truth remains incomplete (1 Cor 13; 9:12) and that it always must be led anew into the truth.

(45)   To receive the truth of God, to witness to it, and to share it belong essentially to the church's reason for existing. In this our churches agree.

They also agree that the reception, recognition, and witness of the truth is the task of the church as a whole, and that in this, various recognition- and witnessing-authorities must work together:

- Holy Scripture

- The handing on of the faith (tradition)

- The witness of the whole people of God (the faithful's *sensus fidei*)

- The church's teaching office *(magisterium)*

- Theology.

The question of how these witnessing authorities are to be understood individually and how they are to be ordered among themselves must be clarified further between our churches.

1.3 Holy Scripture

(46)   Holy Scripture is the original witness of the truth of the living God, which was revealed to us in fullness and clarity in Jesus Christ. "Together we call Holy Scripture *God's word* because in it the witness of the prophets and the apostles, whom God entrusted with his word, is validly brought together. According to the faith of all Christendom, Holy Scripture, in all its parts, in law, prophecy and in the praise of the Psalms, as in the gospel message of the apostles, is about Jesus Christ, *the* word of God for the salvation of the world."[11]

(47)   Together we can say that Holy Scripture was "recorded under the influence of the Holy Spirit."[12] Thus "it is to be affirmed that the books of Scripture firmly, truly and without error teach that truth which God, for the sake of our salvation, wished to have recorded in the holy scriptures."[13] Theology speaks here of the inspiration and inerrancy (infallibility) of Holy Scripture.

(48)   Because Holy Scripture testifies to the word of God, it is the final norm of faith and enjoys the highest honor as the witnessing authority that is closest to revelation. "Together we teach the unsurpassable and irreplaceable authority of Holy Scripture . . . . All of Holy Scripture is to be regarded, by a common conviction, as the *'norma normans non normata':"* the norming, not the normed, norm.[14] It is this because through it, God himself testifies to his truth.[15]

(49)   Due to the truth of God testified to in it, Holy Scripture has established itself in the church from the very beginning and ever anew. This is documented first in the formation of the canon. By differentiating between the canonical and non-canonical writings, the church recognized the prevenient, spirit-worked authority that underlies the writings of the Bible.[16] The ultimate reason for the binding character of the canon is the authority of the word of God, which the church hears in these writings.

(50)   So the Holy Scripture is a book of the church for the church of all generations: "for God's word cannot be without God's people, and conversely, God's people cannot be without God's word."[17] The Bible can never be isolated, but always must be examined in the context of the believing and witnessing communion of the church, which must itself be measured against Holy Scripture.

1.4 The Tradition

(51)   The content of the faith was passed on from generation to generation. In this sense, the church as a whole is a community of tradition. Tradition is thus the church's faithful life within the dynamic of its history, in all statements and actions of the Christian faith, as we find them in the areas of worship, of rite and custom, of art and music. A reduction of tradition to theology or the magisterium would thus be an improper abbreviation of a development of the whole church.

(52)   A distinction should be made here between the communication of the binding apostolic message (*apostolic tradition*—singular!) and the various developments in this message in the life expressions of the church and of individual Christians. The latter are not universally obligatory (*human traditions*—plural!).

(53)   The question of the relationship between Scripture and Tradition has been a long-argued issue between our churches. It can be resolved

today because the Lutheran side acknowledges that Holy Scripture itself comes out of the early Christian tradition and was passed on through the Tradition of the Church.[18] And the Catholic side acknowledges that, despite the high value placed on Tradition, the Holy Scripture sufficiently contains revelation, so that it is not in need of completion (material sufficiency). Therefore, Scripture and Tradition can be neither isolated from one another, nor placed over against one another.

(54) Tradition as the stream of the handing-on of the apostolic faith is therefore not an addition to the substance of Holy Scripture. Rather, tradition, as Scripture interpreted in the Church, is essential for understanding Scripture. This can be seen especially in the confessions and dogmas that are the "answer of faith and at the same time the form of proclamation, that is, the form of the gospel."[19] Together we testify that tradition is a norm that must be confirmed by the normative Holy Scriptures (i.e., a *norma normata*).[20]

(55) The handing down of the witness of the revelation is not a mere passing on of immutable statements, rituals, and customs. Rather, it imparts the experiences, discoveries, and decisions of the church in its thinking and life process in its history with the word of God. The tradition can thus contribute to the greater self-opening of the fullness of God's word. Growing and maturing are life processes of the church and belong to the living tradition of the church. We know, however, that in the lived tradition of our churches, mistaken developments and reductions can and have happened.[21]

(56) As a development of faith, tradition is bound tightly to the respective culture, forms of thought, feelings, experiences, challenges, and conflicts that play a role in determining its concrete shape. The witness of Holy Scripture is the criterion for testing whether the tradition rightly and fully communicates the word of God. The tradition is thus always in need of critical interpretation, just as it is a critical authority for the church. As a medium of the word of God, tradition is a critique of the present church; as an historical medium, it is to be critically questioned on the basis of Scripture. This is valid especially today since both our churches not only live from a common Tradition, but also have separate strands of tradition that each sees as a legitimate development of the original apostolic tradition.

1.5 The Witness of the Whole People of God

(57)   Our churches agree in the conviction that all the baptized participate actively in the transmission of the faith. Baptism grounds participation in the priestly, prophetic, and kingly office of Christ and thereby
establishes the common priesthood of all believers. The totality of believers are promised that, through the presence of the Holy Spirit, they
will remain in the truth.[22]

(58)   In view of the participation of all believers in the transmission of
the faith, the Catholic tradition speaks of "the faith sense of the faithful" *(sensus fidelium)*. With this, it points to the perception and witness
of faith by the whole church. Lutheran theology does not have such a
term, but it has an analogy, on the one hand, in the responsibility of all
believers to give witness to their faith in their respective location and,
on the other hand, in their right and duty to test offered teaching for its
adherence to Scripture. This comprehensive agreement *(magnus consensus)*, which in the Lutheran conception is present in the confession[23]
and is required for common decisions in doctrinal questions, includes
the office of ministry and the community at all levels. Herein lies its
correspondence to the "sense of faith" *(sensus fidei)* that expresses itself
in a universal consensus *(universalis consensus)*.[24]

(59)   The faith sense of the faithful may not be reduced to agreement
with the other recognition- and witnessing-authorities. As a charisma
of the inner agreement with the content of faith, it is itself such an authority through which the church in its fullness recognizes and, in the
course of its life, confesses the content of the faith—in constant interplay with the other recognition- and witnessing-authorities.

(60)   The universal consensus in the sense of faith cannot be determined simply statistically, like a majority decision. It shows itself in a
life that, in the totality of its forms and expressions, testifies to an inner
connection with Christ and, through this, makes Christ known (cf. John
17:24-26, 1 John 5:20). The manifestations of the *sensus fidelium* enrich,
make fruitful, and deepen faith. They act back upon theology and ministerial office and can correct them. Conversely, it is the task of theology
and ministerial office to differentiate between a healthy "sense of faith"
and time-bound trends, false developments, and abridgements of
Christian faith and life (cf. Acts 20:29-31).

1.6 Ministerial Office *(Magisterium)*

(61)   In the Lutheran/Catholic dialogue, a shared recognition has often been affirmed that there is a binding character to Christian doctrine that obligates the church, and that ministerial office in both churches and on both the congregational and supra-congregational level bears a responsibility for teaching.[25] Likewise, the recognition has been shared that the teaching responsibility of the office is bound up with the faith witness of the whole church and that this authoritative teaching stands under the norm of the gospel.[26] In both churches, this mandate of binding teaching is carried out by the authorities empowered for this mandate. The office handed over in ordination has a special responsibility in this regard.[27]

(62)   Agreement also exists between the Lutheran and the Roman Catholic churches that the church as a whole remains in the truth. "We are both of the conviction that the church is held in the truth by the word of God because the Holy Spirit is promised to it, which leads it into all truth."[28] However, this does not exclude that there can be errors in the struggle for the truth.

(63)   In addition to these basic agreements, there is the still unsolved controversy between our churches about who bears this teaching office. This "touches on the question whether the infallibility of faith promised to the church as a whole comes to expression and is mediated through certain structures (college of bishops, council, pope) that have been established in the Church by Christ and therefore under certain conditions can make infallible decisions."[29]

(64)   If one avoids all the misunderstandings and reservations in this complex of questions, then the following core issue in the problem remains:

(65)   According to *Catholic* theology and practice, the highest binding (authentic) teaching office is entrusted to the bishops and to the pope. This office serves the proclamation of the gospel and the nurture of faith and is determined and limited by this task. The bearers of these offices have the right and the duty to proclaim with authority the doctrine they discern. Because of this mandate and this authority, they deserve a "religiously based obedience" from the faithful.[30]

(66)   According to *Lutheran* understanding, the church fulfills its responsibility for doctrine positively through scripturally sound teaching and critically and regulatively through its watch over doctrinal purity.[31] The teaching office in this sense is fulfilled in "a many-layered process, aiming for consensus through the participation of various responsibility-bearers":[32] the bishops, whose job it is "to judge doctrine and to reject doctrine that is contrary to the gospel";[33] the theological teachers of the church; the pastors; and the congregations, whose right and duty it is "to test whether the proclamation offered to them accords with the gospel."[34] This ordered cooperation of ordained and non-ordained congregation members seeks a comprehensive agreement *(magnus consensus)* that has always to prove itself in relation to the continuity of the preaching and teaching tradition of the church. In this sense, all members of the church, according to their respective callings, take part in the responsibility of teaching.

(67)   The controversy over "infallibility" is to be understood in connection with these two conceptions. According to *Catholic* conviction, the teaching office of the bishops and of the pope is equipped, under certain exact, predetermined conditions, with the prerogative of infallibility. *From the Lutheran side,* doctrinal decisions are dependent on recognition by the congregations *(reception)* and are fundamentally open to testing against Holy Scripture. The maintenance of the church in the truth is here "not bound to a certain process or to an always pre-existing authority."[35]

(68)   These two standpoints touch on deeply rooted fundamental convictions. For further efforts at reconciliation, this must be taken into account. *Lutherans* believe that Holy Scripture itself, based on the promise of God, has the power to present the truth of God effectively and to interpret itself *(Autopistie)*. In the *Catholic* church, the authenticity and inerrancy of the church's teaching office is itself an object of faith. Neither of the two partners in this dialogue can expect that the other give up its faith position. A feasible way of addressing these differences appears in defusing the contradictions, so that they are no long church-dividing. In this, one would need to begin from the power of the word of God to interpret itself, which, in a modified form, is also a part of Catholic faith.[36] *On the Catholic side,* it would have to be shown in theory and praxis that the authentic and (under certain circumstances) inerrant teaching office is also an instrument of God[37] that, by the leading of the

Holy Spirit, serves the accomplishment of the Spirit's truth in the church and thus does not stand against the power of Holy Scripture to interpret itself. If *on the Lutheran side* it is possible to understand this Catholic conception as not opposed to the power of the word of God to interpret itself *(Autopistie)*, further opportunities for understanding open themselves up.[38]

1.7 Theology

(69) Persons can only give their answer of faith to the word of God when they responsibly and justifiably recognize that this word and no other is their salvation. Thus the scholarly striving for a rational understanding of revelation in its truth is an important function in the community of believers itself. The task of theology is, by means of methodologically exact argumentation, to identify as much as possible the foundation of faith that in itself is not at our disposal, to formulate the content of faith for contemporary life, and to present it in context. In this task lies the independent right of theology as a witnessing authority of the word of God. The task of the correct recognition and contemporary presentation of faith makes theology necessary and at the same time conditions its connection to the church. In its responsibility for right doctrine, theology is related to the other witnessing authorities and draws from them. Out of the privileged position of Scripture over the other witnessing authorities grows the task of theology to test each of them repeatedly for their accuracy according to the measure of Scripture.

(70) Thereby, theology is afforded a critical role in the church. It must be conscious of the humanly conditioned reductions and distortions in the communication of the revealed truth and correct them to the best of its ability. This needs to occur with the consciousness that theology itself works under the conditions of human fallibility and thus has a duty to be self-critical. The plurality that always exists in theology is conditioned by the variety of biblical writings, the varied nature of humans, their gifts, and their conditions for understanding. Our knowledge is thus partial.

(71) Theology is not only a communicating and interpreting authority, but also has the task to actualize the content of faith, to penetrate it scientifically, and to make it ecumenically fruitful—in the freedom of faith

and in the openness of disciplined inquiry. Certainly there can be tensions between theology and the other witnessing authorities. However, theology remains in all its varied forms always obliged to uphold the unity of the faith within the church.[39]

1.8 Interaction of the Witnessing Authorities

(72) Each of the five witnessing authorities named so far has an independent and thus non-transferable and non-replaceable task. In the church's communion of faith, they are ordered to each other and dependent on one another. They condition one another and affect each other, each in its own specific character.

- *Holy Scripture* is the first and fundamental form of witness of the word of God. It is the unsurpassable norm for the church, for church proclamation, and for faith. Thus, all other witnessing authorities must bindingly orient themselves to Scripture, insofar as they interpret it, more deeply probe it, relate it to the respective situation, and make it fruitful for the Christian life.

- The *Tradition* preserves the living interaction of the faith community with the word of God in the past, for the present, and for the future. As interpretation of the word of God, it is normed by Scripture, but it also must be brought into relation to the church today: to its teaching office, to its theology, and to the sense of faith of today's believers.

- The *sense of faith of the faithful* serves above all the transmission of the gospel to future generations.[40] It has its own weight. It recognizes and confesses the faith, whose norm is Scripture, whose form the Tradition has shaped, to which the teaching office openly witnesses, and that theology critically clarifies. The meaning of the sense of faith among the faithful reveals itself powerfully in the witness of the saints.

- The *church's teaching office,* in the various forms in which it is exercised in our churches by the empowered authorities, has the task of preserving the content of the word of God through interpretation and proclamation, defending against errors, and so serving unity. This teaching office stands under the word of God and may only interpret the Scripture and thus hand on the apostolic tradition. For this, the teaching office is in need of scholarly theology, the impulse of the faithful, and the reception of its decisions through these.[41]

- The accurate, contemporary, and methodologically critical comprehension and presentation of the truth of revelation and faith belong to *scholarly theology*. For this reason, theology as a science is especially dependent on the interaction with the other witnessing authorities. It is to derive and set forth its contents from Scripture and tradition, from the witness both of the teaching office and of the whole people of God. In addition, it attends to insights from non-theological disciplines and is open for dialog with non-Christian religions.

(73) The described interaction of the witnessing authorities can only succeed through the movement of the Holy Spirit and cannot be understood without this movement. "The distribution of graces and offices is effected by the Spirit, enriching the Church of Jesus Christ with different functions 'in order to equip the saints for the work of service, so as to build up the body of Christ' (Eph 4:12)."[42] So the interactions that in fact take place in the church are more numerous and diverse than can be shown here. That is the common conviction of our churches.

The interplay of the individual witnessing authorities, even within the churches, is not without tensions and conflicts, and is thus in need of ordered rules. Moreover, as confessionally pointed assertions come to light, their opposition must be allayed through the exchange of ecumenical experiences and in mutual trust in the effectiveness of the Spirit.

2. Sacraments

(74)   In the understanding of Baptism and, above all, of the Eucharist, the dialogue between our churches has led to far-reaching commonalities.[43] In relation to the remaining open questions regarding the concept of sacraments and the number of sacraments, the theme "Communion of Saints" offers viewpoints that lead us even further.

2.1 Sacraments as Means of Communion with Christ and with One Another

(75)   The communion that God grants us humans is not immediate, but rather—as the Catholic and Lutheran traditions commonly emphasize—

is mediated by external-bodily means: through the word and the sacraments. In the sacraments, the relation to communion is expressed in a specific way. This can be seen above all in that, according to the New Testament, Baptism and the Lord's Supper effect membership in the body of Christ and growth in him (1 Cor 12:13; 10:17). The communion of believers thus bases itself on participation in the one Lord Jesus, and not on the identity of race, nation, gender, social origin, education, or sympathy. The sacraments thus present the nature of the communion of the church, the communion of saints.

2.2 The Institution of the Sacraments

(76)   We both teach that the church does not have the means of grace from itself but has received them from her Lord and is to administer them loyally. These means of grace are based in the word and work of Jesus Christ, the crucified and risen Lord, as they are testified to in the New Testament. He who established the church also gave it the necessary means for its life. We both teach that the church, under the impulse of the Holy Spirit, unfolds in its life what the Lord has given it.

2.3 Christ as the Giver within the Sacraments

(77)   Together we teach that Jesus Christ is the actual giver within the sacraments. When the church acts in accord with the sacrament's institution, the Lord himself is present,[44] sharing himself with his people and giving them his gifts. Those who fulfill the ministry of administering and distributing the sacraments act "in representation of Christ."[45]

2.4 The Activity of the Holy Spirit in the Sacraments

(78)   Christ is active in the church through the Holy Spirit (cf. John 14:26; 16:13ff.). The Holy Spirit is the one who through the sacraments—as through the word—"calls, gathers, enlightens, and makes holy the whole Christian church on earth and keeps it with Jesus Christ in the one common, true faith."[46] Since this activity of the Holy Spirit does not occur "by my own understanding or strength,"[47] it is appropriate to pray for the Holy Spirit (cf. Luke 11:13). This comes to expression in the epiclesis, the prayer for the Holy Spirit, that has been discovered anew in the ecumenical dialogue, with an appeal to ancient (especially Eastern) church tradition.[48]

2.5 The Concept and Number of the Sacraments

(79)   The concept "sacrament," as generally used in the present, does not occur in the New Testament, but essential elements are present there that later become tied to this concept. The Greek word *mysterion,* which in the first centuries of Christianity was often used in association with the Latin word *sacramentum,* was originally not directly related to actions with signs, which later were called sacraments.

(80)   Augustine was the first to use the term "sacrament" in the sense of an all-encompassing general concept of Christian signs of salvation: sacraments are visible signs of an invisible reality.[49] Prior to mid-twelfth century, there was no definitive agreement about the term or the number of sacraments in either the Western or the Eastern church. The number and ordering of the sacraments was first set in the High and Late Scholastic Periods,[50] as they were later defended and permanently defined at Trent[51] by the Roman Catholic *magisterium* against the attacks of the Reformation.

(81)   Historical findings themselves suggest that too much dogmatic weight should not be given to the controversial theological questions related to the number of the sacraments. Reformation theology also had no original interest in setting a defined number of sacraments.

(82)   When the *Roman Catholic Church*—as the Orthodox churches—counts seven sacraments, then this enumeration is to be understood as an expression of fullness. In the sacraments, God's grace reaches humans at existentially meaningful points in their lives. Catholic theology also recognizes differences between individual sacraments, in relation to the situations in which they are celebrated, as well as in relation to the gifts that they mediate. Baptism and the Lord's Supper are distinguished as major sacraments *(sacramenta majora).* The other sacraments *(sacramenta minora)* are related to them, for in every sacrament life with Christ is developed, a life that is grounded in Baptism and whose source and center is the Eucharist.[52]

(83)   The *Lutheran Church* affirms and practices corresponding liturgical acts in particular life situations: Confirmation, Marriage, Blessing of the Sick (with anointing).[53] It understands them as acts of blessing. It differentiates them from Baptism and the Lord's Supper and sees them

as oriented toward Baptism and the Supper. The Lutheran Church considers it appropriate to emphasize the fundamental significance of Baptism and the Lord's Supper by the term "sacrament." The confession of sin, because of the efficacious pronouncement of forgiveness (absolution), is also counted among the sacraments in the Augsburg Confession[54] and in the Apology.[55] Although this inclusion of confession among the sacraments has not generally survived, the sacramental character of the word of absolution is beyond question. Moreover, the Apology weighs the possibility of employing the term "sacrament" for other church practices, e.g., for ordination.[56] The Lutheran Church has thus neither conclusively defined its own understanding of the sacraments, nor condemned other understandings.[57] It therefore does not consider the use of the term "sacrament" in a more far-reaching sense by other churches to be church-dividing.

(84) Together, we can say:

1. Baptism and the Lord's Supper stand out because of their fundamental significance for the reception of salvation and for membership in the body of Christ.

2. The other liturgical actions which the Roman Catholic Church considers sacraments and the corresponding liturgical actions in the Lutheran Church are oriented toward Baptism and the Lord's Supper.

(85) The question of what weight should be given to the differing uses of the terms "sacrament" and "act of blessing" needs more reflection on the basis of studies that have already been completed.[58] It would be wise here to deal with the individual practices on the basis of their historical developments, liturgical forms, and theological understandings. This path could lead to a differentiated concept of sacraments that could be the basis of consensus.

3. The Church as Sign and Instrument of Salvation[59]

(86) Together we confess that Jesus Christ, true God and true human, is the primal sacrament, in whom the living God shares himself with humanity. Through the means of grace, in which Christ works by the power of the Holy Spirit, the faithful receive a share in the communion

of love that exists in God's very self. In this sense, the church is "the people made one by the unity of the Father and the Son and the Holy Spirit."[60] God desires to use the church to draw people of all times and places into communion with himself.

(87) This definition of the church is expressed in Vatican II as follows: "The Church is in Christ like *(veluti)* a sacrament or as a sign and instrument both of a very closely knit union with God and of the unity of the whole human race."[61] The term "sacrament" is used here analogically.[62] It is intended to express both the radical dependence of the church on the triune God and its universal commission. So it is clear that the church does not have its purpose and goal in itself, that is, it does not exist from and for itself. Only in and through Christ, only in and through the Holy Spirit is the church effective as a means of salvation.[63] In this sense, recent Catholic theology has used the term "fundamental sacrament" in reference to the church. The use of this term serves to illustrate that the church, although it is the body of Christ, may not simply be identified with Christ, the "primal sacrament." The church is taken into service by him to share salvation with all people and is in need of the constant, enlivening power of the Holy Spirit. It must "unceasingly pursue repentance and renewal."[64]

(88) According to the *Lutheran* conception, the church is the community in which the God-ordained means of grace—word and sacrament—become effective for the people. Thus the church has, in a derived sense, the character of an instrument of salvation: as mediator of word and sacrament, it is the instrument through which the Holy Spirit makes people holy. It is "the mother that begets and bears every Christian through the word of God."[65] Although the salvation-effecting activity of God and the mediating activity of the church come together in this event, they are nonetheless clearly different. It is the church, to be sure, that communicates to believers their share in salvation, but only Christ, who brought about salvation for the world, gives believers a share in this salvation through word and sacrament. Therefore it corresponds to Lutheran theology to apply the term "sacrament," alongside of its use for Baptism and the Lord's Supper, to Jesus Christ, as did Augustine,[66] rather than to the church. Because Christ establishes and maintains the church through the individual sacraments, it is important in Lutheran theology clearly to distinguish Catholic language about the church as "sacrament" from the use of this term for the individual

sacraments. Moreover, Lutheran theology is concerned that the use of the concept of sacrament in relation to the church might obscure that the church is both holy and sinful at the same time.

(89)   Together we can state the following:

1. The church is a creation of the Word *(creatura verbi)* and at the same time servant of the word *(ministra verbi)*, which it has received.[67]

2. The church is in its entire existence a sign of the saving will of God,[68] who desires "that all people be saved and come to see the truth" (1 Tim 2:4).

3. The church, as mediator of word and sacrament, is an instrument of grace.

4. The church is shaped in its very essence by the reception and the administration of word and sacrament.

5. The church remains constantly subject to the Lord, and salvation remains a gift of God, even in the work of the church. In this sense, the relationship of Christ and church is defined by the conjunction of unity and diversity.

Where this is together taught, there is a material agreement, even if different judgments exist about the analogous use of the term "sacrament" in relationship to the church.

Notes

[1] Second Vatican Council, Constitution on the Sacred Liturgy, *Sacrosanctum concilium* (SC), par. 7: "He is present through his power in the sacraments; thus, when anyone baptizes, Christ himself is baptizing. He is present through his word, in that he himself is speaking when scripture is read in church."

[2] SC, 59.

[3] In *The Book of Concord: The Confessions of the Evangelical Lutheran Church,* Robert Kolb and Timothy J. Wengert, eds. p. 46 (Minneapolis: Fortress Press, 2000).

[4] CA 7; Kolb and Wengert, 42.

[5] Cp. LG, 1.

[6] Second Vatican Council, Dogmatic Constitution on Divine Revelation, *Dei verbum* (DV), par. 4.

[7] DV 5; cf. Luther, Small Catechism, arti. 3.

[8] Cf. KWS, par. 15.

[9] KWS, par. 15.

[10] Cf. KWS, par. 13.

[11] KWS, par. 12.

[12] DV, 11; cf. Formula of Concord, Epitome (FC Ep), Summary, 1 (Kolb and Wengert, 486).

[13] DV, 11.

[14] KWS, par. 12.

[15] Cf. *Verbindliches Zeugnis,* vol. 1. Kanon—Schrift—Tradition, Wolfhart Pannenberg & Theodor Schneider, eds. (Göttingen: Vandenhoeck & Ruprecht, 1992).

[16] Cf. KWS, par. 12.

[17] Martin Luther, *On the Councils and the Church,* in *Luther's Works* (LW), vol. 41 (Philadelphia: Fortress Press, 1966) 150; WA 50, 629.

[18] Cf. KWS, par. 12b, and *The Gospel and the Church,* in *Growth in Agreement: Reports and Agreed Statements of Ecumenical Conversations on a World Level,* Harding Meyer & Lukas Vischer, eds. (New York: Paulist Press, 1984), par. 16.

[19] Cf. KWS, par. 15; cf. ibid., pars. 10–19.

[20] Cf. FC, Ep. Summary, 2, 7, 8 (Kolb & Wengert, 486f.); FC, SD, Summary, 10 (Kolb & Wengert, 526).

[21] Congregation for the Doctrine of the Faith, Declaration *Mysterium ecclesiae* (1975), par. 5, in *Vatican Council II: More Postconciliar Documents,* Austin Flannery, ed., 433 (Northport, NY: Costello Publishing, 1982).

[22] LG, 12, 37.

[23] CA 1 (Kolb and Wengert, 37).

[24] LG, 12.

[25] Cf. *The Ministry in the Church,* par. 57, in *Growth in Agreement,* 266.

[26] Ibid.; *Facing Unity,* par. 60, in *Growth in Agreement II: Reports and Agreed Statements of Ecumenical Conversations on a World Level, 1982–1998,* Jeffrey Gros, Harding Meyer, and William G. Rusch, eds. (Geneva: WCC Publications, 2000) 457f.; KWS, par. 13.

[27] Cf. KWS, par. 76.

[28] KWS, par. 13; *The Ministry in the Church,* par. 58 (in *Growth in Agreement,* 266).

[29] Cf. KWS, par. 13; also par. 76.

[30] LG, 25.

[31] *Lehrordnung der VELKD von 16.6.1956.* Erklärung zur Lehrverpflichtung und Handhabung der Lehrgewalt, I: Recht und Verlautbarungen, Martin Lindow, ed. (Hanover, 1989), no. 470.

[32] *Kirchliches Leben in ökumenischer Verpflichtung,* edited by Hermann Brandt (Stuttgart: Calwer Verlag, 1989), 102.

[33] CA 28:21.

[34] Lehrordnung der VELKD vom 16.6.1956, no. 470; cf. CA 28:22f.

[35] *Kirchliches Leben in ökumenischer Verpflichtung,* 133.

[36] Cf. Pontifical Biblical Commission, *The Interpretation of the Bible in the Church,* in *Origins,* 23 (1994), sec. III,B,3, par. 115.

[37] Cf. DV, 1–6, 11, 21.

[38] Cf. *Verbindliches Zeugnis,* 392f.

[39] Cf. KWS, par. 18; UR, 9, also 5.

[40] DV, 8; LG, 12.

[41] Cf. DV, 10.

[42] UR, 2.

[43] *The Ministry in the Church;* KWS, par. 24–42; *Condemnations of the Reformation Era,* 84–117.

[44] Cf. FC SD 7.76; cf. SC 7: Christ "is present through his power in the sacraments; thus, when anyone baptizes, Christ himself is baptizing."

[45] Cf. Apol. 7:28, "When they offer the word of Christ or the sacraments, they offer them in the stead and place of Christ."

[46] Small Catechism, Creed, 6.

[47] Small Catechism, Creed, 6.

[48] SC, 6, states in relation to the celebration of the Eucharist that all occurs "through the power of the Holy Spirit." The Decree on the Apostolate of the Laity, *Apostolicam actuositatem* (AA), 3, states that the Holy Spirit "works the sanctification of God's people through ministry and sacrament." Cf. *The Eucharist*, pars. 21–24.

[49] Cf. *Patrologia Latina*, 32:1410; 33:527.

[50] The Bull of Union for the Armenians (1439) of the Council of Florence sets these forth explicitly (DH 1310).

[51] Cf. DH 1601: Baptism *(baptisma)*, confirmation *(confirmatio)*, the Eucharist *(eucharistia)*, penance *(paenitentia)*, anointing of the sick *(extrema unctio)*, ordination *(ordo)*, and marriage *(matrimonium)*.

[52] LG, 11; PO, 5.

[53] Cf. *Agende für lutherische Kirchen und Gemeinden III*, Kirchenleitung der VELKD, ed., part 2, Marriage Service (1988); part 4, Service with the Ill (1994); part 6, Confirmation (1999). [Trans.: for comparable American Lutheran services, see *Lutheran Book of Worship* (Minneapolis: Augsburg, 1978) 198–205.]

[54] Cf. the relations among CA 9–13.

[55] Apol. 13:4.

[56] Apol. 13:11-13.

[57] Cf. Apol. 13:17: "No intelligent person will argue much about the number or the terminology, as long as those things are retained that have the mandate and promises of God." Cf. also *Lehrverurteilungen in Gespräch*.

[58] KWS, pars. 20f., 43–51, *Condemnations of the Reformation Era*, 72–84, 117–45.

[59] Cf. *Church and Justification*, pars. 118–30.

[60] LG, 4.

[61] LG, 1.

[62] This is indicated by *veluti* in LG 1.

[63] Cf. KWS, par. 43.

[64] LG, 8; cf. 48.

[65] Large Catechism, Creed, 42.

[66] Augustine, Epistle 187; cf. *Church and Justification*, par. 128.

[67] KWS, par. 13.

[68] Cf. also LG, 1.

Chapter 5

The Communion of
Those Sanctified by Grace

1. The Communion of Justified Sinners

(90) The communion of saints is the communion of justified sinners. At the present time our churches are able to testify that "a basic consensus exists in the doctrine of the justification of the sinner."[1] They are also agreed that this doctrine is not just one part of the Christian doctrine of faith, but that it is a critical standard for the church "for testing at all times whether its proclamation and its praxis correspond to what has been given to it by its Lord."[2]

(91) The ecumenical significance of this agreement is seen in the role the doctrine of justification played as the decisive doctrinal teaching over which the unity of the Western church was broken in the sixteenth century. The Reformers recognized in this teaching the core of Christian doctrine as a whole. Thus the denial of this teaching by the dominant theology and church of that time meant for them that Christ's honor and his benefits were being "obscured."[3] Conversely, the Council of Trent saw in the Reformer's teaching on justification "a serious blow to the unity of the church."[4]

(92) These mutual condemnations have, according to the judgment of both our churches today, lost their church-dividing effect.[5]

2. The Biblical Message of Justification

(93)   The fundamental agreement is above all evident in the shared understanding of the biblical message about justification.

(94)   Its roots lie in the *Old Testament*: God grants his righteousness (i.e., his faithfulness to the covenant) to Israel, God's elected people, in that God makes himself known to Israel as the one who is "merciful and gracious . . . abounding in steadfast love and faithfulness" (Exod 34:6). Likewise Israel is to be righteous, in that it is to remain completely loyal to the Lord its God (Deut 18:13) and to "love the Lord your God with all your heart, and with all your soul, and with all your might" (Deut 6:5).

(95)   *Jesus* proclaimed the reign of this God whose eschatological and eternal kingdom was now breaking in (Mark 1:4). He announces God's salvation to the poor, to the hungry, to the weeping, and to those persecuted by their enemies (Luke 6:20-23). Through his proclamation about the God who seeks out the lost (Luke 15) and his table fellowship with "tax collectors and sinners," he calls sinners to repentance, includes them into his fellowship, and thereby gives them an inheritance in the kingdom of God (Mark 2:17). Likewise he calls his disciples to live a righteousness that "exceeds" that of those who teach the Law and are faithful to it among the contemporary people of Israel: a radical and unlimited love for the neighbor, even for the enemy (Matt 5:43-48), a love that corresponds to God's love (Luke 10:25-37; Matt 25:31-46). Jesus himself lives this kind of love among his disciples, in that he, their Master, serves them (Luke 22:24-27).

(96)   In obedience to the will of God (Mark 14:36), Jesus gave his life on the cross for the salvation of humankind from sin, death, and the devil (Mark 10:45; 14:24). In Jesus' resurrection from death, God gave this love an eternal victory and raised him to be Lord over all (Phil 2:6-11). Whoever believes in him and is baptized in his name (Mark 16:16) has a part in the life of the Risen One and thereby in God's eternal salvation (Rom 10:9f.; Acts 16:31). Through the gift of the Holy Spirit (Acts 2:38f) as the power by which God raised Christ from the dead (Rom 1:4; 8:11), the baptized are freed from their sins and sanctified before God (1 Cor 6:11) and are called to a life in sanctification (1 Thess 4:3) and righteousness (Rom 6:15). In the Lord's Supper they partake in the body and

blood of Christ who gave himself for them and lives for them (1 Cor 10:16f.; 15:3-5).

(97)   According to the apostle *Paul* our justification occurs on the basis of Christ's death and resurrection. God shows his righteousness to persons by making them righteous by virtue of their faith in the crucified and risen Christ (Rom 3:25). The whole of the gospel of salvation finds here its center (Rom 1:16f.). The justification of the sinner is a gift of God's grace. No human being can be justified by his or her own works (Eph 2:8-10). Faith in Christ bestows justification on the sinner (Rom 3:28). For it is Christ alone who frees us from the wrath of God and the deadly power of sin over our lives (Rom 8:34; Acts 4:12), and it is God's Spirit alone that empowers us to live in righteousness (Gal 3:1-5). Being in Christ is a "new creation" (2 Cor 5:17).

(98)   This saving message of the gospel contradicts any confidence in the salvific benefits of "works of the Law" (Gal 2:16) as well as any kind of boasting before God (1 Cor 1:29; 3:21; 4:7). The Law is indeed God's Law and as such is "holy and just and good" (Rom 7:12). But because all are sinners, all are under God's judgment (Rom 3:9-20) through the Law (Gal 3:13). They cannot free themselves from sin by fulfilling the commandments of the Law and claim God's righteousness on the basis of their own works (Rom 4:1-8).

(99)   Those who have been saved from sin by God's grace in Jesus Christ and who have become justified through faith in him should conform to this new reality also in their lives. They cannot live in sin any longer (Rom 6:1), but, precisely because they no longer live under the Law but under grace (Rom 6:15), they are enabled and obligated to live in righteousness through the power of the Holy Spirit (Rom 8:12f.). In Christ Jesus, faith unfolds its power as "faith working in love" (Gal 5:6). All Christian action and conduct are therefore the "fruit of the Spirit" (Gal 5:22f) and thereby the fulfillment of the Law (1 Cor 7:19) in living out the commandment of love (Gal 5:14; Rom 13:8-10).

   In this sense justification encompasses sanctification (1 Cor 6–11), faith is made known in obedience (Rom 1:5), and freedom from the Law leads to fulfillment of the Law (Gal 5:13f).

(100)   Justification affects individuals so radically that they are transformed in their innermost being (Titus 3:4-7: *rebirth*). It is *their* sins that

are forgiven and *their* lives that are utterly new in Christ. It is *their* faith in which Jesus is confessed as their Lord (Rom 10:9f) and with which they stand or fall (2 Cor 4:4). This faith is joined intimately with conscience (2 Cor 1:2; Rom 14:2). And because Jesus Christ is the one Lord of all Christians (Rom 10:12), justification places the individual believer into the church as the communion of saints. The faith confessed at baptism is the faith of all Christians (1 Cor 15:11). The baptism received makes one a member of the body of Christ (1 Cor 12:12f.; Eph 4:4-6). The Lord's Supper grants a common share in the body and blood of Christ and, in turn, communion with all Christians (1 Cor 19:16f.).

(101)   By means of the gospel of justification through faith and "apart from the Law" (Rom 3:21), God brings Jew and Gentile together in Jesus Christ into the fellowship of the children of God (Gal 4:6f.; Rom 3:14-17). The former division between Jew and Gentile is overcome in Jesus Christ (Rom 1:16; 10:12f.): As children of Adam all are sinners— for them all the crucified and risen Christ has become the new Adam (Rom 5:12-21), who unifies them through faith and baptism into his body (Eph 2:13-17). The one Spirit of God is so at work in them all with the Spirit's power and gifts that they serve one another as members of the one Body of Christ (1 Cor 12; Phil 2:1-11). So the one gospel of justification in Jesus Christ brings into existence one church of Jews and Gentiles as God's eschatological community of salvation (Eph 3:3-5), which lives together as the communion of saints through the working of the one Spirit of God (1 Cor 1:2).

(102)   With the doctrine of justification the apostle Paul brings to expression what he has recognized as the decisive content of the gospel. By this he not only evoked much hostility within Judaism (1 Thess 2:14-16), but he also aroused much opposition within the church (Gal 2:11ff.). But because the message of justification was decisively for him "the truth of the gospel" (Gal 1:6-9), he saw it as his apostolic duty to do everything he could to reach consensus on this matter with the other apostles (Gal 2:2: "in order to make sure that I was not running, or had not run, in vain"; and, in essence, 1 Cor 15:11). The acceptance of precisely his controversial letters into the canon of the New Testament shows that the church recognized Paul's doctrine of justification as a binding interpretation of the one gospel of Christ for the whole church.

(103)   The New Testament contains texts in which the same gospel is proclaimed and interpreted in a different way so that aspects of faith are brought to bear that are not so centrally developed in Paul's letters. Particularly in the gospels, the preaching, teaching, and deeds of Jesus as well as the history of his Passion stand at the center.

(104)   Thus *Matthew,* for example, emphasizes the impending judgment according to works that Jesus' disciples themselves must face, a judgment by which the chaff will be separated from the wheat within the church (cf. Matt 13:24-30, 36-43; 21:11-13, 24-25). The standard for this judgment will be what we have done or not done for "the least of Jesus' brothers and sisters" (Matt 25:31-46), whether we have forgiven one another (Matt 18:21-35; 6:14). This corresponds essentially to what Paul teaches (cf. 2 Cor 5:10; 1 Cor 13; Col 3:13). The disciples' obligation to fulfill all the commandments of the Law and thereby to exceed the Pharisees and scribes (Matt 5:17-20), as well as the admonition of the Letter of James about a faith without works (Jas 2:14-26), are to be viewed as "warning signals" for the interpretation in the church of the Pauline doctrine of justification.

(105)   In his portrait of Jesus, *Luke* emphasizes especially those characteristics that mark Jesus as the Savior of sinners. He brings together three parables in chapter 15 that speak of the saving love of God for the lost under the leitmotif of the joy in heaven over every sinner who repents and turns to the kingdom of God (Luke 15:7, 10, 24, 32). Luke transmits the parable of the Pharisee and the taxcollector (Luke 18:9-14). He tells of the taxcollector Zacchaeus whom Jesus greets with the statement: "The Son of Man came to seek out and to save the lost" (Luke 19:10). And he reports that Simon Peter, at his first meeting with Jesus, falls on his knees with the words: "Go away from me, Lord, for I am a sinful man" (Luke 5:8).

(106)   A quite unique context of theological interpretation of the gospel is found in the Gospel of John and the Letter to the Hebrews. Both emphasize the central significance of the incarnation (John 1:1-8; Heb 2:1-18) and the exaltation and glorification of Jesus (John 17; Heb 1:3-13; 4:14-16).

(107)   True faith according to *John* sees in the man Jesus the Son sent from God who throughout his earthly ministry is one with the Father

(John 10:30; 14:8-11) and in whose post-Easter/eternal fellowship of
love with the Father the disciples find an abiding home through the
Holy Spirit (John 17:20-26, 14:16f., 26; 15:26; 16:7-15). By believing in
Jesus and in keeping his words, his disciples participate in eternal life
already in their earthly lives (John 3:18; 5:24-27; 6:47f.; 11:25f.).

(108)   According to the Letter to the Hebrews, Jesus' obedient suffering (Heb 5:7-10), his humiliation unto death (Heb 13:13), and his journey through death by crucifixion to the heavenly throne of God have
priestly significance (Heb 4:14-16; 9:11-14). The way of the church is
discipleship along this path on which the eternal high priest has gone
before her (Heb 4:14-16; 10:19-25; 12:1f.; 13:9-16). On this path Christians unite themselves with the fathers and mothers of Israel as the
wandering people of God (Heb 11:1-40). The goal of this earthly pilgrimage is to be united with the heavenly communion of saints and the
choir of angels (Heb 12:18-24).

This is also the great promise of the Revelation of John.

(109)   This development of the message about Christ must be brought
to bear in the church along with the Pauline doctrine of justification and
must shape its faith and life. In order to see the New Testament writings
together in this sense, the church needs the ever new help of the Spirit of
God. That the justification of the sinner by grace through faith, as proclaimed by Paul, is here the decisive key is an insight has been emphasized
in the Western church especially through the influence of Augustine.
The Eastern church has been shaped more strongly by the theology of
the Johannine writings and the Letter to the Hebrews.

3. The Common Witness of Justification

(110)   Today our two churches share a fundamental agreement in the
understanding of the biblical message of justification. On this basis the
oppositions that arose in the sixteenth century about the doctrines of
justification and sanctification can be overcome—despite still existing
differences. The Reformers, attending to the experience of the still sinful existence of Christians, emphasized the comforting power of the
gospel; more strongly than Paul, they made a distinction between the
righteousness pronounced in justification and sanctification. The pre-
vailing Catholic theology feared here a neglect of sanctification and

stressed the transforming character of justifying grace. The *Joint Declaration on the Doctrine of Justification* from the Lutheran World Federation and the Pontifical Council for Promoting of Christian Unity interrelates these differences as different accents and thereby brings to expression a common understanding of the doctrine of justification.[6]

Together we can say:

(111)   Justification is a creative action of the Triune God. In the crucifixion and resurrection of Jesus Christ God accomplishes the salvation of the sinner by grace alone. This salvation cannot be earned or merited through human works but is received and accepted only by faith in Jesus Christ through the power of the Holy Spirit.

(112)   In the Holy Spirit, given in the proclamation of the gospel and in the sacrament of baptism, believers receive a share in the relationship of the crucified and risen Son with the Father.

(113)   Justification, which works forgiveness of sins, never becomes an event of the past; faith receives it always anew in trust and obedience and is certain of it. Sanctification remains always a work and gift of grace; it does not proceed from our own resources and is never owned like a possession at our disposal. Faith is that personal "Yes" spoken by the Christian; life in sanctification is the Christian's life-long obedience.

(114)   Because of sin, unbelief, doubt, and anxiety, believers always remain temptable and tempted. Christian living takes place in constant spiritual battle, only so can it mature and grow. Throughout their lives, Christians ever again need forgiveness and healing. They can only live "according to the Spirit" and can only resist the temptations to live "according to the flesh" by seeking forgiveness, healing, and support in Christ and offering themselves totally in love to his Spirit. In this sense justified and sanctified Christians are "sinners and righteous," unholy and holy "at the same time."

(115)   In order to remain in sanctification and to grow in it, repentance is needed anew always. The possibility of the confession of sins and the absolution from sins is an important aid in this. The center of the justified and sanctified life is fellowship with Christ and one another in the Lord's Supper. This Christian life is practiced daily in listening to the

word of God in the Holy Scriptures and in prayer as devotion to the Lord in petition, praise, and thanksgiving.

(116)   Justified by God, the person now stands in a unique relationship to God. In addition, the person is numbered among the members of the church, the body of Christ. Nowhere else can humans be so deeply and completely bound to one another as in Christ and in his church as the communion of saints. Thus, the sanctification given to and enjoined upon individual Christians is bound up with the sanctification of all Christians, of the entire holy church, in which they participate through their life in the local congregation. Especially in their worship they are tied to the communion of the saints of the church in every time and place.

4. The Significance of the Message of Justification for Church and World

(117)   According to the conviction of our churches, the message of justification has central significance for the total doctrine, life, and ordering of the churches. A basic agreement in the doctrine of justification and sanctification must therefore result in an understanding of the church as the "communion of saints" and in a corresponding communion between our two churches.

(118)   Because justification by God's grace is able to give the entire life of faithful persons an unshakeable foundation of trust, new possibilities for a common witness in the world are opened for our churches by this basic agreement.[7]

(119)   The more confusing the variety of religious and pseudo-religious options in our world becomes, the more important it is that our churches publicly bear witness together to the love of God for all people. The more an atmosphere of vanishing trust toward one another spreads throughout our society, the more helpful it will be for many uncertain people seeking support and help if Christians are able to speak with one voice, with personal certainty of faith, about the unchanging and limitless faithfulness of God with regard to his promises of salvation.

(120)   The agreement in the understanding of the gospel as the message of the justification of the sinner by God's grace can enable our

churches to speak convincingly of the liberating power of the forgiveness of God in a public arena where guilt is always taboo. If even serious personal guilt can be confessed before God without the guilty
losing their personal worth, then it may also be possible for human beings in leading positions in politics, economics, medicine, law, and the
media publicly to take responsibility for mistakes and guilt. It will
therefore be a service of public pastoral care if our churches together
encourage an honest and lasting remembrance of the heinous deeds
that have been committed in the history of our people.

(121) In a time when many persons who have become accustomed to
a growing prosperity are required to cut back their personal expecta-
tions and demands, faith is able to liberate from both arrogance and
self-reproach because God gives human beings their dignity without
regard to persons or their accomplishments. This dignity does not
measure itself according to the societal norms of living standards and
career. It is also not lost when, due to external causes or through their
own personal situation, people find themselves in difficult circumstances in which they experience social exclusion and thereby are
shaken in their sense of self-worth.

(122) In a time when the fabric of society threatens to unravel, the appeal to social conscience gains in importance. If the church understands itself as a sign for the promised unity of humanity, Christians
have a special responsibility for solidarity in society. The churches can
offer their special contribution all the more convincingly, the more suc-
cessful they are in presenting a unified witness to the message of the
love of Christ.

Notes

[1] Response of the German Bishops Conference to *Condemnations of the Reformation Era*, 9; Response of the VELKD on this document, Conclusion 4.1.1.

[2] *Condemnations of the Reformation Era*, 69; cf. also JDDJ, par. 18.

[3] Apology 4:2; Smalcald Articles 2:1.

[4] DH 1520.

[5] Cf. JDDJ, par. 41.

[6] JDDJ, par. 40.

[7] Cf. Wort des Rates der EKD und der Deutschen Bischofskonferenz zur wirtschaft-
lichen und sozialen Lage in Deutschland: Für eine Zukunft in Solidarität und Gerech-
tigkeit: Gemeinsame Texte 9 (1997).

Chapter 6

The Communion of Those Called to Service

1. Common Calling of All Members

(123)   The communion of saints, justified and sanctified by grace through word and sacrament, is called to serve God and humankind. This applies to the community as a whole as well as to each individual member. Through Holy Baptism, individuals are made members of the people of God, gifted with the gifts of the Spirit and called to love God and the neighbor.[1] "Baptism incorporates each believer into the people of God's new covenant and makes of them a universal priesthood—an instrument of his purpose for the whole creation."[2]

(124)   The calling that occurs in baptism is understood in the New Testament—in connection with Exodus 19:5ff.—as a calling to priesthood. Thus in the earliest Christian communities, the following word was spoken to the newly baptized: "Like living stones, let yourselves be built into a spiritual house, to be a holy priesthood, to offer spiritual sacrifices acceptable to God through Jesus Christ . . . . But you are a chosen race, a royal priesthood, a holy nation, God's own people, in order that you may proclaim the mighty acts of him who called you out of darkness into his marvelous light" (1 Pet 2:5, 9).

(125)   The common priesthood of all the baptized includes the whole Christian life: the area of worship, where Christians "offer a sacrifice of praise to God, that is, the fruit of lips that confess his name" (Heb 13:15); the proclamation of the mighty acts of God, prayer for all people

(1 Tim 2:1), as well as life witness in the everyday. In all of this, they present themselves "as a living sacrifice, holy and acceptable to God" (Rom 12:1). This can even lead to the giving of one's life in martyrdom, for which precisely in the twentieth century there are numerous examples in all traditions. "In this way, Christ can be experienced and understood by the world through the service of the whole church. The people of God are called priestly because they live out of the sacrifice of Christ and are taken into this sacrifice. Dedication to God and neighbor—that is the service of the priesthood of all believers."[3]

(126) The comprehensive call of the whole people of God is characterized in recent church documents with reference to the three-fold office of Christ—priestly, prophetic, and kingly.[4] In the Catholic baptismal liturgy, "the celebrant anoints the newly baptized with chrism, for whoever is baptized belongs to Christ, and is, like him, 'anointed' to the office of priest, king, and prophet."[5] "All are called and sent to give prophetic witness to the gospel of Jesus Christ, to celebrate the liturgy together and to serve humankind."[6] The life and faith experience of many Christians is needed so that witness can be given to the gospel in the various areas of life.

(127) The common calling of all Christians to the "kingly priesthood" has not been taught clearly in all periods of church history.[7] In medieval theology, the difference between cleric and lay was emphasized in such a way that the equality of all believers receded into the background. The Reformation took a stand against this emphasis on a privileged spiritual estate. In its teaching of the priesthood of all believers, it emphasized the equal dignity of all the baptized and the immediate access of each individual believer to God. In the debate between the confessional movements, the concept of the "common priesthood" was seen as differentiating the two sides. It was at times interpreted, both by its proponents and its opponents, as calling into question the ordained office.

(128) On the *Catholic* side, Vatican II caused a breakthrough on this question. In its teaching of a "common priesthood of all believers," it clearly emphasized the equal dignity of all Christians: "the chosen people of God is one: 'one Lord, one faith, one baptism' (Eph 4:5); sharing a common dignity as members from their regeneration in Christ, having the same filial grace and the same vocation to perfection; possessing

in common one salvation, one hope and one undivided charity."[8] Even the office of ministry is encompassed by this equality: "if by the will of Christ some are made teachers, pastors and dispensers of mysteries on behalf of others, yet all share a true equality with regard to the dignity and to the activity common to all the faithful for the building up of the Body of Christ."[9]

(129) Today, we can together declare this "true equality in the dignity common to all the faithful."[10] In its description of the calling of the whole people of God, Vatican II speaks of the "common priesthood of all believers."

(130) On the *Lutheran* side, a "priesthood of all baptized" or a "priesthood of all believers" is spoken of: "Since the right to stand before God as a priest is based on one's baptism, one can speak of a 'priesthood of all baptized.' Since this right is claimed in faith, one can speak of a 'priesthood of all believers.'"[11]

The common witness to this priesthood is of great ecumenical significance. "The doctrine of the common priesthood of all the baptized and of the serving character of the ministries in the church and for the church represents in our day *a joint starting point* for Lutherans and Catholics in their attempt to clarify as yet open problems regarding the understanding of the ordained ministry in the church."[12]

(131) The relationship between the common priesthood of all believers and the ordained ministry requires more precise definition. Vatican II offers the following: "The common priesthood of the faithful and the ministerial or hierarchical priesthood, though they differ from one another in essence and not only in degree, are nonetheless interrelated: each of them in its own special way is a participation in the one priesthood of Christ."[13] That is to say: all of the baptized participate in the common priesthood. Some of these are called beyond this to the special priestly office that Christ established for the church. This office is not an intensified level of the common priesthood. The grace of justification is the same for all Christians. Whenever one speaks of the grace of the office, then it is about the call and grace for service to word and sacrament.[14] "While the common priesthood of the faithful is exercised by the unfolding of baptismal grace—a life of faith, hope, and charity, a life according to the Spirit—the ministerial priesthood is at the service of the common priesthood. It is directed at the unfolding of the baptismal grace of all

Christians. The ministerial priesthood is a means by which Christ unceasingly builds up and leads his Church."[15] Moreover, the ordained also are charged with the development of the grace of baptism in all aspects of their life. In order to express the relationship between the special priesthood and the common priesthood, Vatican II quotes Augustine: "For you I am bishop, with you I am a Christian. The first denotes duty, the latter grace, the first denotes danger, the latter salvation."[16]

(132)   In the document *Communion in Word and Sacrament*, the relationship between the common priesthood and the special ministry was seen as a "question that had not been clarified satisfactorily."[17] The response of the United Evangelical Lutheran Church of Germany and the German National Committee of the Lutheran World Federation to the document *Condemnations of the Reformation Era: Do They Still Divide?* states what we can both affirm: "While the proclamation of the gospel to one another is a matter for all Christians, proclamation in the public realm of the church—i.e., the public, oral proclamation and the administration of the (by their nature public) sacraments of Baptism and the Lord's Supper—presumes that a Christian is called, blessed, and sent by the church to this service in the commission of Christ, as occurs in ordination.[18] Herein lies the basic difference between the ordained office and the common priesthood. The office is not established as delegated from the congregation . . ."; it has its foundation "in the call to proclamation by Jesus Christ himself,[19] who aims not only to win individuals, but also to build up the Church."[20]

(133)   The common priesthood of all baptized must also prove itself in everyday life: "We are called as members of Christ's body to follow him—entering obediently into the structures of this world to witness to the Lord who is already there."[21]

(134)   The responsibility that Christians take on for the world expresses itself especially in social action and in prayer. "As citizens they must cooperate with other citizens with their own particular skill and on their own responsibility. Everywhere and in all things they must seek the justice of God's kingdom . . . . Preeminent among the works of this type of apostolate is that of Christian social action."[22] In worship and in personal prayer, especially in intercessory prayer, Christians bring the world and its manifold problems before God and ask him for mercy. In this way, Christians intercede as priests for other people. Martin Luther

saw here a high dignity of Christians: "Not only are we the freest of kings, we are also priests forever, which is far more excellent than being kings, for as priests we are worthy to appear before God to pray for others and to teach one another divine things. These are the functions of priests, and they cannot be granted to any unbeliever. Thus Christ has made it possible for us, provided we believe in him, to be not only his brethren, co-heirs, and fellow-kings, but also his fellow-priests."[23]

(135)   The service of the priesthood of all believers is carried out in many ways. "As sharers in the office of Christ as priest, prophet, and king, the laity have an active part to play in the life and action of the Church. Their activity is so necessary within the church communities that without it the apostolate of the pastors is often unable to achieve its full effectiveness. . . . They refresh the spirit of pastors and of the rest of the faithful. . . . They bring to the Church people who perhaps are far removed from it, earnestly cooperate in presenting the word of God especially by means of catechetical instruction."[24] That which is said here for the Catholic Church is also valid for the Lutheran churches. In our churches, voluntary, part-time, and full-time workers on various levels of church life work together, also in the area of worship and proclamation.[25]

2. Special Gifts, Ministries, and Offices in the New Testament

(136)   The church does not exist on the basis of a decision by its first members, but rather on the basis of its calling by Jesus Christ. In his earthly actions, Jesus called people to follow him as his disciples. Out of them, he chose twelve to be by his side. He sent them out to proclaim the gospel and gave them a share in his authority. As the resurrected Lord, he renewed their sending. They were enabled, by the communication of the Holy Spirit, to go throughout the world as his witnesses and to proclaim the gospel to the nations. Thus, the crowd of followers called into discipleship became the worldwide church of Jesus Christ.

(137)   Beyond the foundational events of Pentecost, the path of the church is defined by a varied bestowal of the gifts of the Spirit. The church builds itself in every one of its congregations through the varied gifts of the Spirit that their members have received in Baptism and faith. These are, according to 1 Corinthians 12, the *charisms*, which present themselves not only in extraordinary abilities, but much more, ac-

cording to the teaching of the apostle, as "ministries" that should serve the building up of the community. As the various members work together, the community should grow as the "body of Christ" and be, as it were, the presence of the Holy Spirit in the concrete life-space of the world. Among the "charismatic ministries," the offices of the apostles, prophets, and teachers are of fundamental significance (1 Cor 12:28).

(138)   Extending Paul's early letters, the Letter to the *Ephesians* emphasizes the fundamental significance of offices as ministries for the church and its congregations. The church carries out its mission in an internally structured form (Eph 4:7-16). The called office-bearers (apostles, prophets, evangelists, pastors, and teachers) are there for the faithful, to "equip them for the work of ministry, for the building up of the body of Christ" (v. 12).

The ministerial offices are thus gifts *(charisms)* of the risen Christ to his church. The community received them and shaped them. The Letter to the Ephesians witnesses to a theologically reflected congregational order that connects the developed condition of the church in the late first century with the apostolic beginnings. "Built on the foundation of apostles and prophets" (2:20), the church fulfills its mission in its time. The Pastoral Epistles and the letters of Peter show how it not only preserved the "apostolic heritage," but also permitted its effectiveness to develop.

(139)   The structure of the church in the time of the apostles, to which the post-apostolic church appeals, was more diverse than can be seen in the Acts of the Apostles.

At the beginning, two different types of congregational structure had clearly developed:

- in the Jewish-Christian area of Palestine, the presbyter structure, in Jerusalem with James at the helm (cf. Acts 15);

- in the Jewish-Christian/Gentile-Christian realm around Antioch, the more pneumatologically grounded structure with the leading offices of apostle, prophet, and teacher (cf. Acts 13:1-2; 1 Cor 12:28). Philippians 1:1, with its mention of *episkopoi* and *diakonoi*, presents its own, place-specific formation.

(140)   In an overview of the development of congregational order and offices in the early era, a certain variety can be seen, open to further development. In the various situations and under the various conditions

of the early church, the one mission and the one ministry are actualized. The mission and the ministry of the gospel both belong to the self-understanding of the apostolic office, as Paul already early reflects theologically in his letters.

(141)   The basic elements of a theology of office also arise out of the apostolic self-understanding of Paul. These elements are especially clear in the theological profile of the apostolic office, as presented in 2 Corinthians 5:18-20:

- The ministry of the apostle is a "ministry of reconciliation." As such, it is based on the reconciliation that God has completed for all time in Jesus Christ. In the proclamation of the gospel through the apostle, God's reconciliation is communicated to "us" and to all humanity.

- In his calling, the apostle is entrusted with the "word of reconciliation." He carries out the ministry to which he is appointed "in Christ's stead": Christ is the one who, through the apostle, proclaims and acts.

- The ministry of the apostle, as also of those that work with him, is responsible cooperation in the building up of the *ekklesia* of God on earth.

(142)   The office of apostle becomes the ideal image of ministerial office for the church. From this, the idea of an apostolic succession *(successio apostolica)* becomes effective in the early church and, in an elemental way, even in the New Testament:

- As eyewitnesses to the Risen One, the apostles have a unique and fundamental significance. They proclaim Christ as the "foundation that is lain" (1 Cor 3:11) in a way that is normative for the church of all ages. The ministry of the apostles to the gospel and to the congregations is transferred to successors whose ministry is measured by the content of the foundational proclamation of the apostles.

- The transfer of the ministry to successors happens through the biblical word of sending, through the laying on of hands and prayer (Acts 6:6; 1 Tim 4:14ff.; 2 Tim 1:6). Through this, the gifts of the Spirit are effectively passed on which enable one to fulfill the office. Thus, the one appointed for ministry comes into a special relationship to the master of this ministry, Jesus Christ; a relationship that encompasses and forms his whole life.

This document does not introduce any independent teaching about the ministerial office of the church. It presumes the explanations that have been achieved in the previous dialogues and extends them in view of the *communio*-structure of the church.

3. Communion of Communions

(143)   Communion with the Triune God that is mediated by word and sacrament is realized concretely in the local churches. In them, unity can be experienced as an essential characteristic of the church, in that all natural, dividing differences are sublimated in the common participation in the goods God gives.

(144)   This unity of the faithful and the baptized with God and one another is the basis for the universality *(catholicity)* of the church. Individuals encounter the *communio* in the Eucharistic community in which they live and, at the same time, they are bound together with the other Eucharistic communities. The individuals, for their part, contribute to this community. "Accordingly, Lutherans and Catholics see the church of God in local, regional and universal terms, but these different ways in which the church becomes reality must be understood on the basis of the one holy catholic and apostolic church, the *una sancta* of the creed."[26] This means that just as the universal Church is not a union, addition, or confederation of the individual (particular) churches, so also the particular churches are not a subsequent administrative partitioning of the *una sancta* in individual regions and provinces.[27]

(145)   In the first centuries the church presents itself as the *communio ecclesiarum,* i.e., as a network individual local churches bound by manifold relationships, whose unity is expressed in gathering with the bishop around the Eucharistic altar. Several local churches came together around the apostolic sees and formed patriarchates. Although in later centuries organizational and centralizing tendencies, especially in the West, limited the variety of communion, the *communio* of the bishop-led church remained the fundamental shape of the church's existence and order.

(146)   Together we are of the conviction that the communion given in Christ must be visible. From history we know of various forms of expressing *communio:* confessions of faith, synodical letters, correspondence between local churches on the occasion of festivals and for mutual information, Eucharistic letters of exhortation, prayer for one another, collegial meetings and collegial cooperation of bishops (particularly in the councils), mutual visits and hospitality. Church divisions were expressed by the refusal of these signs of *communio.* It is a sign of growing communion that many of these expressions of communion are practiced again today between our churches.

(147)   New forms have also developed between our churches: mutual invitations and words of greeting, councils of churches and other forms of cooperation, common prayer and common worship, common consecrations and rituals of blessing, conferences, common social and diaconal work, common spiritual words and statements on public issues, dialogues on doctrinal questions, etc. Forms have developed that serve an ecumenical community that has grown but is not yet complete.

(148)   In the more exact definition of the relationship of local and regional churches to the universal church, differences can nonetheless be seen between Lutheran and Catholic ecclesiology.

(149)   According to *Lutheran understanding,* the local congregation in its worship is the central realization of the Church. In the proclamation of the word and in the celebration of the sacraments, as in the office that serves them, the Lutheran congregation has what is decisive, what makes it church. In this local event, the "one holy church" of the confession of faith is present. The communion given in Christ with all other believers and baptized Christians from other local congregations finds its expression in the clustering of local congregations into larger communities on regional, national, and universal levels. The *communio* in these larger communities becomes concrete in the agreed understanding of the apostolic faith, through communion in the sacraments, and in the mutual recognition of office. This pulpit, altar, and ministry fellowship is constitutive for the Lutheran understanding of the churchly *koinonia* on all levels. It is served by various institutional structures, whereby the bishops, the community of the ordained clergy, and the synods together have a special responsibility for unity.

(150) Also according to *Catholic understanding*, in the local church the whole church is present. By "local church," however, is understood the unity of the local congregations under the bishop;[28] the local congregation is recognized as a local form of expression of the diocese and of the whole church.[29] Because the entire church exists both in and from individual particular churches, these particular churches are not simply branches of the total church, nor can they exist for themselves as isolated bodies. It is essential that they stand in communion with the other local churches as also with the church as a whole. This communion finds its particular expression in the *communio hierarchica*, i.e., in the communion of bishops with one another and with the pope as their head. So the bishop is the representative of the whole church in his diocese and, at the same time, he is the representative of the diocese in relation to all other dioceses.[30]

(151) The differences make it clear that the Lutheran/Catholic dialogue over the church has a basis in the common vision of the Church as *communio,* but that it must take up the classic controversial question about the structures of episcopacy and primacy in the church.

(152) We can now say together that the ecclesial communion that occurs in the local gathering around word and sacrament as communion with God and one another, while not the whole church, is wholly church. It is thus included in the universal church as the communion of all local churches. In relation both to this universal communion and to the respective local churches, the creed speaks of a "una sancta catholica et apostolica ecclesia" as a spiritual reality.

4. The Petrine Ministry

(153) To serve the unity of the church, which is as a communion of communions, is an essential task of ministerial office.[31] In this context the question arises of whether and in what way this ministry also will and must be exercised for the universal unity of the church. The New Testament witnesses to the special function and task of the apostle Peter. Thus the ministry of unity also is defined as "Petrine Ministry." This ministry as an enduring element in the church of Christ has found respect and living expression since the earliest times. Nonetheless, in the course of history, controversies arose over particular structures and forms of this expression.

(154)   According to the *Roman Catholic understanding*, the *communion* among the local churches and their bishops has "its point of reference in the communion with the church of Rome and the bishop of Rome as the holder of the chair of Peter."[32] At least since the First Vatican Council, the jurisdictional and doctrinal primacy of the pope, essentially though not in all its concrete forms, has been an integral and indelible part of Roman Catholic doctrine. Other churches often saw and still see the papacy as the greatest obstacle on the path toward the unity of the church. The critical statements of the Reformation's confessional writings seem to exclude any agreement on the papacy. Pope Paul VI said in a speech before the Secretariat for the Promotion of Christian Unity in 1967: "The pope, as we all know, is undoubtedly the gravest obstacle in the path of ecumenism."[33] In his encyclical *Ut unum sint* [1995], Pope John Paul II on the one hand affirmed the Roman Catholic understanding of primacy and on the other invited an open discussion about the forms in which the office is exercised.[34]

4.1 The Petrine Office as Object of Dialogue

(155)   The inter-confessional dialog turned first to the themes on which an agreement seemed most likely. The experience that extensive agreement was possible in controversial topics—e.g., on the doctrine of justification, on the Lord's Supper, and in part also on ministerial office—led on the same basis to the introduction into the dialogue of the office of the pope. In the international Lutheran/Roman Catholic dialogue, this has so far only occurred in the framework of other topics.[35]

(156)   Primacy became an independent topic for the first time in the Lutheran/Roman Catholic dialogue in the United States. The dialogue group prepared the 1974 report *Papal Primacy and the Universal Church*. In Germany, aspects of this topic also have been explored, as can be seen in the first report of the German Bilateral Working Group *Communion in Word and Sacrament* from 1984[36] and in the document *Condemnations of the Reformation Era* of 1985.[37]

(157)   In the conviction that the ministry to universal unity must be exercised and that an agreement on the question of the office of Peter is of great importance for the communion of our churches, we seek to determine how far our agreements reach at the present moment, where further controversies exist, and what weight these controversies have for our future path.

4.2 Peter in the New Testament

(158)   Simon belongs to the first three disciples whom Jesus called (Mark 1:16-20; cf. Luke 5:1-10). In the group of twelve, he is ascribed an outstanding significance, expressed in the epithets Jesus gives him: Cephas (Aramaic) = Peter (Greek) = "Rock" (Mark 3:6). The sense of this name is expanded upon in Matthew 16:18: to his confession "you are the Messiah, the Son of the living God", Jesus answers: "However, I say to you: you are Peter, and on this rock I will build my Church, and the powers of the underworld will not conquer it. I will give you the keys to the kingdom of heaven; what you bind on earth will be bound in heaven, and what you loose on earth, will also be loosed in heaven."

(159)   By the "power of the keys" that Jesus hands over to Peter is meant the authority, with which come a special responsibility, to open heaven to humanity (cf. Matt 23:13). It is illustrated by the image of binding and loosing. The authority that is handed over to all the disciples in Matthew 18:18 is to be understood in the context of Matthew 18's community order; it is the authority within the church to judge errors against God's command and to forgive sins (church discipline). More comprehensively, however, apostolic authority and responsibility relates to the opening of the saving way of Jesus for all humanity. This can be seen in John 20:23 and Matthew 28:18-20, with Jesus' dual mandate to his disciples to baptize and to teach his commands to all, so that discipleship of Jesus may be possible for them. As the Jewish background of the image of binding and loosing suggests, the authority to decide about true and false teaching also comes along with this.

(160)   Simon is not "the Rock" on the basis of human qualities. Certainly he loyally followed his Lord and belongs to his most trusted disciples (Mark 9:2-8). He was also the first to declare Jesus to be the Messiah (Mark 8:27-30). At the beginning of the Passion, he was still convinced of the steadfastness of his discipleship (Mark. 14:29). And yet, soon after this he denies being a disciple three times (Mark. 14:54-62). That the Lord still renews his original call (John 21:15-17) was understood in the earliest church as special evidence of grace: Christ's grace alone gives Peter immovable permanence as the "rock" of his church.

(161)   With his Pentecost sermon (Acts 2:14-36), Peter steps forward as the first disciple into the public light with the proclamation of the

gospel. Also, according to the witness of Acts, Peter was the first disciple to win a non-Jew for the faith and baptize him (Acts 10:1-11, 18). For a time, he leads the original church in Jerusalem along with John and James, the brother of Jesus. At the Apostolic Council, his vote has special weight and contributes decisively to the fundamental acceptance of one church of Jews and Gentiles: "The grace of the Lord Jesus" allows all Christians to experience together the one salvation of God (Acts 15:7-11). For Paul, communion with Peter was important (Gal 1:19; 2:9), and he finds it unbearable when Peter, of all people, does not behave in accordance with the gospel on a decisive issue (Gal 2:11ff.).

(162)   The Synoptic Gospels show the church's lively memory of Simon Peter as "spokesman" for the Twelve (Mark 9:5; 10:28; John 6:66-68; Matt 17:24) and as specifically commissioned by Christ to strengthen his brother disciples (Luke 22:31f.). As the "apostle of Jesus Christ", Peter became a central authority for a range of congregations (especially 1 Peter and 2 Peter).

(163)   As spokesman for the apostles, Peter gave the decisive confession to Jesus as the Christ (i.e., Messiah), which is the foundation for the Church of all times (cf. 1 Cor 3:11). Here and in Jesus' answer (Matt. 16:17), Peter's pre-Easter significance is seen as one with the special authorization he received from the Risen One in his appearance (1 Cor 15:5; John 21:15-17). The statements in the New Testament about Peter show that the early church combined with the figure of Peter the functions of a teaching and pastoral ministry that relate to all congregations and that particularly facilitate their unity. Herein lies the present challenge: to think together in our ecumenical dealings in a totally new way about a Petrine Ministry for the whole church.

4.3 Forms of the Petrine Ministry in the History of Theology and the Church

(164)   After establishing ourselves biblically in regard to the Petrine Ministry, a contemporary awareness of its historical development is a further prerequisite in our dialogue in order to understand its ecclesiological significance. Obviously, this development can in this context only be presented in its overarching features and in great simplification.

(165) The connection of Peter with Rome results from his living in Rome at the end of his life and dying there as a martyr, according to ancient church tradition (cf. 1 Clement 5:4). He is seen as the first bishop of Rome. The centuries-long process out of which developed the understanding of the Roman bishop as the representative of the Petrine Ministry was influenced most of all by three factors:

1. *theologically,* by the predominant model of the church;

2. *pastorally,* by the relationship of the bishop of Rome to the other bishops in the Church;

3. *politically,* by the constellations in which the church lived immediately in time and space.

(166) One can delineate three periods in church history that each brought characteristic traits into the image of the office of Peter. They overlap with one another structurally in such a way that the defining moments of the earlier epoch are validated in the epoch or epochs to follow, even if often in opposition to reigning opinion. Individually, one can distinguish:

1. the post-apostolic period until the fourth century;

2. the period from the fourth century until the First Vatican Council and its reception (middle of the twentieth century);

3. The Second Vatican Council and the debate over its documents, which continues up to the present.

(167) The image of the church in the *first period* is the model of the *communio* in the shape local congregations, with equal rights in principle, in a relation of spiritual and organizational exchange.[38] For the preservation of the true Christian faith in the whole church, it became necessary to find fixed points of unity. As such points, those churches whose beginnings are marked by an apostle were of special significance *(sedes apostolica).* Among these churches, the congregation in Rome took on a special position, recognized since the second century.[39] It protected the graves of Peter and Paul and thus possessed a double apostolicity. Out of this initially spiritual significance of their see, the Roman bishops since the end of the second century derived a responsibility for the whole Church. In other churches, this led at first to resistance (e.g., in

the controversy of Easter and the baptism of heretics), but Rome none-theless had established itself as the center of *communio* by the beginning of the fourth century at the latest. This asserted role in the framework of the solidarity of the whole Church was not justified juridically, how-ever, but through the special authority of a faith judgment made by a possessor of a *sedes apostolica*, which in principle belongs to every member of the college of bishops.

Factually, the significance of Rome was all the greater because it was an imperial capital and the only apostolic see in the West.

(168)   The great turning point that introduces the *second period* is the in-clusion of the church into the structure of the Roman Empire, accom-plished by the Emperors Constantine [313] and Theodosius [380]. Many political and administrative tasks were thereby granted to the bishops in general and especially to the bishop of the capital city of the (West-ern) empire, particularly since the unity of the faith was seen as the in-dispensable foundation for the state. Along with the leaders of the other patriarchal sees, the bishop of Rome is called "pope" from the fourth century on, but ever more exclusively since the end of antiquity.[40] More and more, his office becomes not just the guarantor of the apostolic tra-dition, but also the church's legislator, claiming not just authority *(auc-toritas)*, but also power *(potestas)*. Since the beginning of the fifth century at the latest, the claim of the bishop of Rome is derived expressly from the succession of the apostle Peter, including the authorities granted to him according to Matthew 16:16-18. In place of a local principle *(sedes apostolica)*, a personal principle appears *(successor Petri)*. The structural elements that appear here are strongly extended in the following cen-turies. The theological climax of this development is the First Vatican Council. In individual detail, the following phases can be differentiated.

(169)   In the dogmatic disputes of the fourth and fifth centuries and their crises for the church (e.g., in the Arian controversy), the theologi-cal position of Rome is increasingly perceived as normative and deci-sive. This is seen especially clearly in the influence at the Council of Chalcedon (451) of the Tome of Leo, a letter of Pope Leo the Great. Even the East recognized that controversies affecting the whole church can-not be solved definitively against the pope. However, in regard to the difficult questions that arose in the East, Rome sometimes lacked an in-tuitive feeling for the issues. As a result, a certain emotional reserve toward the Pope developed in the East. The Roman Bishop's claim to

primacy on the one hand, and on the other, the political claims of the patriarchate of Constantinople, bishop of the contemporary capital of the empire, along with other causes, led to an alienation between the churches of the East and the West in the second half of the first millennium. In 1054, communion between the two was formally broken.

(170)   In the medieval West, the papacy was widely seen as the foundation and origin of all authority in the church. Various factors contributed to this view, for example:

- the conviction of the Germanic nations of the outstanding significance of St. Peter as the guardian of heaven's gate, passed on to his successors;

- the recognition of the Pseudo-Isidorian Decrees of around 850, with their weakening of the power of metropolitans (the responsibility of the pope for every bishop);

- the disintegration of collegiality among bishops in the constant, often warring disputes among the imperial and independent bishops who belonged to the nobility;

- the conflicts between bishops and cathedral chapters.

In the ecclesiological imagination, the leading image of the *communio* receded behind that of the church as the "body of Christ." Unlike as with Paul, however, the horizontal elements were not given prominence (the mutual support of the members of the body, the necessity of every individual member). Rather, the vertical structures were emphasized most strongly: the essential member is the head, from which the life currents flow. In heaven this is Christ; on earth, however, it is the pope. The pope ascribed to himself exclusively the title of the *vicarius Christi*,[41] which until then was attributed to all the bishops and even to the king. Rome understood itself now not only as the center, but as the point of departure and origin *(fons et origo)* of all newly developed local churches. The pope stood in a certain sense "over against" the rest of the church. This development was furthered by the eleventh century struggle of the Gregorian reformers for the freedom of the church against the threat of an imperial "nationalization" of the church.[42] In reality, however, the pope came to see himself as parallel to the emperor. Roman papalism corresponded to the imperial centralized power, as was most sharply expressed in the bull *Unam Sanctam* by Boniface VIII (1302).[43]

(171)   Nevertheless, at no time did the church become a closed papal system. Through the "heresy clause," known since the ninth century, a theoretical openness was maintained: despite the conviction, on the one hand, of the absolute position of the pope (*Prima sedes a nemine iudicatur*—the pope is judged by no one),[44] the possibility was acknowledged that the pope might become schismatic or heretical (*"papa a fide devius"*—a pope who deviates from the faith).[45] The pope himself cannot decide whether such has occurred; only the rest of the church has this power. Opinions differed on just how this might be determined. The emergency situation of the Western Schism in the fourteenth and fifteenth centuries, with at times three popes, showed that the bishop of Rome and the other bishops remained interrelated (Council of Constance). Finally, it must be taken into account that, given the limited communications of the time, the difference between papal theory and the independence of local churches was often considerable.

(172)   In the controversies of the Reformation and the Counter-reformation, as also in the modern struggles with secularism in all of its forms, the papacy has become for Roman Catholic Christians the outstanding marker of their own identity. In the face of growing insecurity, the pope has become the guarantor of the religious need for security for many Catholics, who come to feel emotionally bound to him. In some cases, the pope has become a defender against a state's absolute or arbitrary use of power.

(173)   For a time, various state or national churches as well as episcopal currents, as least according to their intention, acted as counterbalances to papal absolutism. Elements of the *communio* ecclesiology played a role in this. With the destruction of the *ancien Regime* in the French Revolution of 1789 and in Germany after the secularization, these counterbalances fell away. In the aftermath, attention was concentrated less on the already uncontroversial primacy of jurisdiction, than on the pope's doctrinal primacy, according to which he was seen no longer as a qualified witness to faith charged with the ministry of *testificatio fidei,* but, even more strongly than in the Middle Ages, as the judge of faith with the duty of *determinatio fidei.* Along these lines, the attention of the First Vatican Council (1869–1870) was concentrated on the named prerogatives of the papal office that, primarily due to external reasons, came to be isolated from the context of the council's ecclesiology and were de-

fined as faith-binding dogmas (primacy of jurisdiction and infallibility of the Roman pope). The fact should not be overlooked, however, that it was the intention of the council, in defining infallibility, to bind the Pope to the faith and proclamation of the whole church. At the same time, it sought to distinguish him as the final arbiter in cases of conflict so that the church might remain in the truth.[46] In the following period, papalist tendencies grew within the church, on the one hand, while on the other, especially between the two world wars (ca. 1920–1940), the elements of *communio,* of reception by the church, and of the faithful's sense of the faith *(sensus fidelium)* were again taken up in a turn to the wider tradition of theology (beyond the neo-scholastic view from the Middle Ages).

(174)   In the Second Vatican Council (1962–1965), a third period began, in so far as for the first time the church itself is expressly made the theme of a general church gathering. The constitution *Lumen gentium* took up the numerous biblical images for the church, with particular significance laid on the term "people of God." At the same time, the ancient church's understanding of *communio,* with its emphasis of the local churches and of the collegial office of the bishop, experienced a renewed evaluation. The leading image of the body of Christ was not excluded, but remained as of equal importance. Two images of the church that complement each other in substance, but remain in tension due to their loaded history, now receive conciliar authority. This has consequences also for the theology of the papacy: within the *communio* model, the pope and the College of Bishops stand in principle in a more vital and necessary polarity to and with one another. Within the *hierarchy* model, the Pope remains the absolute point of relation for bishops. According to the "Preliminary explanatory note," par. 4, to the constitution *Lumen gentium,* he can, "as the supreme shepherd of the Church, exercise at any time his full authority at his discretion *(ad placitum),* as is demanded by his office."[47]

(175)   This problematic, not resolved at the council, has since prompted discussion within the Roman Catholic Church as well as in the ecumenical community.[48] It has become clear to those who favor a strong position for the papal office that critical situations cannot be mastered by papal authority alone. Rather, efforts toward a consensus of the whole church are needed, which, as church history shows, does not necessarily come about without conflict.

4.4 The Reformers' Critique of the Papacy

(176)   In the Reformation, the question of justification was the theologically central issue. This question, however, is connected in various ways to ecclesiological questions and thus to the question of the function and authority of the pope. In this context, the papacy was criticized by Luther and the Lutheran Confessional Writings, in three senses.

(177)   The pope, they claimed, had set himself and his authority above the authority of the word of God, as witnessed in Holy Scripture. Luther first found this expressed in the papal approval of the traffic in indulgences. However, Luther and the other Reformers saw this claim also in many other papal measures and laws. Luther judged that the pope had failed his pastoral duty and had led Christians into insecurity. In light of these experiences, the Reformers disputed the claim that obedience to the pope is necessary for salvation.[49] This resistance to the pope, driven by intense need, seemed obligatory.[50] And yet, as late as 1531, Luther could say that he would kiss the pope's feet if he would not hinder the gospel of the grace of God in the church.[51] A few years later, the conviction that Luther had already expressed in 1520[52] had come to dominate: the Antichrist of 2 Thessalonians 2:4 had appeared in the person of the pope.[53]

(178)   The Reformers also elaborated a fundamental critique of the papacy, as they experienced it, on the basis of the essence of the church. They pointed to the ancient church structure, under which the pope was only the bishop of Rome. The bishops, however, were "equal in office," and the pope had at most a certain primacy according to human law.[54] This is why Melanchthon recommended that "concerning the Pope . . . if he would allow the gospel, we, too, may . . . for the sake of peace and general unity . . . grant to him his superiority over the bishops which he has 'by human right.'"[55] On the basis of the New Testament and many witnesses of church history, however, the Reformers found no ground for a spiritual superiority of the pope over other bishops.[56] The image of the rock from Matthew 16:16 is understood in terms of Peter's faith or confession, which precisely does not include a superiority of his person.[57] Luther also can relate this text to Christ.[58] The office of the keys (Matthew 16) and the charge to tend the flock (John 21) are understood as a mandate given to all the apostles through Peter and thus to the church as a whole.[59]

(179)   Finally, the Reformers argued critically that the pope had taken on worldly power alongside the spiritual and therefore had been further untrue to his calling. They pointed to Christ, who did not rule in a worldly manner, but rather had subjected himself to suffering and founded a spiritual reign.[60]

The Reformers countered the claim of the pope manifested in these three points with the biblical witness especially, but also with the history of the early church.

(180)   The development of the Post-Reformation Catholic understanding of the church increasingly made the papacy an important identity marker in Roman Catholic self-understanding. This development had various grounds; Luther's understanding of the gospel was not among its direct causes, but certainly among them was the "ecclesiastical and political effects of his [Luther's] basic concerns in the understanding of church, ministry, and the teaching office."[61] Protestant anti-papal polemics seemed confirmed in the nineteenth century, from the Protestant perspective, in the statements about the papal office of the First Vatican Council.

4.5 Lutheran Questions and Considerations Today

(181)   For the Lutheran understanding, the dogmatic determination of Vatican I that the bishop of Rome enjoys by divine right the highest power of jurisdiction raises today the question whether there could not be other legitimate forms for the ministry to the universal unity of the church. In relation to the definition of papal infallibility in *ex cathedra* decisions, the Lutheran side must ask whether here has been preserved the "reservation of binding character" [*Verbindlichkeitsvorbehalt*] over against all doctrinal decisions of the church, which they see as required by the gospel, a reservation grounded in the self-sovereignty and final binding authority of the gospel. "In the Reformation view the teaching of the church or of a teaching ministry must take place precisely in this dialectical tension between the claim of its binding nature and the reservation relating to that binding nature."[62] In this sense, the ecclesiological problematic has to do with the article of justification.

(182)   Vatican II confirmed the dogmatic statements of Vatican I and at the same time took a broader view of the Church and its official structure as *communio* with the college of bishops. The statement that the

church's teaching office does not stand above the word of God, but is rather to serve it takes up the Reformers' concern for the priority of the biblical witness also in relation to the teaching office of the pope.[63] In the Lutheran view, however, a tension exists here with the related assertion that only the teaching office of the church may authoritatively explain the word of God. Is it not here to be feared that in the necessary "interaction of witnessing authorities,"[64] the weight will fall one-sidedly on the authority of the teaching office and that this is not sufficiently bound together de facto with the other authorities that stand with and before it, especially the witness of Holy Scripture?

(183)   Contemporary Lutheran theology contains new reflections on the question of the papacy. They are facilitated by developments in the Catholic world, i.e., by the reduction of the political power of the Roman see and by intra-Catholic discussions of the papacy and the way popes have exercised their office. Previous dialogues have led to the point that the Reformers' statement that the pope is the Antichrist is today regretted and no longer maintained.[65] The exegetical examination of the figure of Peter in the New Testament as well as of the role of the apostle Paul have allowed the significance of a personal responsibility for the communion and unity of the church to be seen anew.[66]

(184)   Finally, there are insights that concern the essence and structure of the church as *communio*. Alongside the congregational level, the regional and universal dimensions of the church have again entered the consciousness of Lutheran theology. Reflections have been made about what structures are needed on these levels to support church unity. Approaches to the regional office of bishop found in the Lutheran Confessions have been are further developed.[67] It is here understood that the church is a spiritual communion and a human social structure in one, in which institutional and legal elements belong essentially.

(185)   The Reformers' critique is still of paramount importance for the Lutheran churches. Nevertheless, they see the question of the ministry to the universal unity in the church framed in different circumstances today than in the time of the Reformation. Engagement with this question must keep in view the worldwide community of churches in the World Council of Churches and in the Lutheran World Federation, as well as the development that the papacy has undergone since the Reformation. And it must further note that the Lutheran churches them-

selves possess their own tradition in the order and form of their church bodies.

In conclusion, the following can be said today from the Lutheran side on the question of the papacy:

(186)   1. "The church is actualized at different levels: as the local church (congregation), as the church of a larger region or country, and as the universal Church. At each of these levels, albeit in different forms, it is essential that the ministry be both 'in and over-against' the ecclesial community."[68] Thus, the church, "as the assembly of the faithful or saints which lives from God's Word and the sacraments,"[69] has its elementary form of existence in the worshiping celebration of the local congregation and the ministry of the office conferred by ordination is ordered to this event. In this worshiping celebration of the local church, the one church of all times and places is made present.[70]

(187)   2. The church realizes its unity at the regional and universal levels in the full communion *(communio)* of the local or regional churches: in proclamation and teaching, in the celebration of the sacraments, and in the ministry of the office conferred by ordination ordered to this event. This presumes the full mutual recognition of the churches' ministries. This unity has its criterion in the preservation of the apostolic tradition fundamental to the church. The full communion of the churches includes their legitimate, historically developed diversity (in doctrinal form, liturgy, and polity).

(188)   3. Regional and church-wide institutional structures necessarily serve this full communion. The following elements are essential in such structures:

1. the personal responsibility of individuals in offices of leadership;

2. the collegial, communal responsibility of the ordained office-bearers;

3. the synodical responsibility of ordained and non-ordained representatives of the people of God.[71]

For all, baptism lays the foundation of such responsibility. The concrete calling *(vocatio)* to the office of the public proclamation of the word and administration of the sacraments occurs in ordination, which, in its connection to Holy Scripture and the Confessions of the church, is a special sign for the continuity and communion in apostolic succession throughout the ages. Fundamentally, the whole church stands in this continuity, but it is most clear in the ordained ministry. The ordained office-bearers have a collegial responsibility for the regional church and for the whole church. The handing on of this personal responsibility for the whole occurs with the participation of representatives of other regional churches and of the worldwide communion. Synodical responsibility is given generally by vote and commitment; the synods represent the communion of the ordained and the non-ordained. The responsibility for the unity of the church lies with all of them.

(189)   4. The personal responsibility for the whole at the regional level generally lies with the bishop's office. In communion with it, other leaders in church office assume regional responsibility in their areas. Corresponding to this, it also should be considered whether, according to Lutheran understanding, a church-wide Petrine Ministry is appropriate, possible, or even necessary. Its task would be to care for the maintaining of the universal church in the apostolic truth and for the world-wide full communion of churches, and likewise, to encourage local and regional churches in faith and ministry (cf. Luke 22:32). In this sense, it would have a pastoral task toward all churches and would be at the same time their representative.

(190)   5. The detailed constitutional or canonical form of such a church-wide Petrine Ministry can be conceived in different ways. Among the necessary criteria would be: its obligation to the collegial and synodical structures of responsibility at the church's universal level, as well as respect for the variety and relative independence of the regional churches. Church-wide unity would then be a "conciliar communion" of all churches in "reconciled diversity" with a Petrine Ministry that serves this community. It would not have a centralized legal form. The doctrinal responsibility of the church-wide Petrine Ministry, which consists above all in care for the truth to be determined in new situations *(determinatio fidei)*, would have to rest on the common responsibility of the people of God for the truth *(communicatio fidei)* and be oriented toward reception by the people of God. In everything, it must at the same time recognize the superiority of biblical truth.

(191) 6. The connection of such a universal Petrine Ministry to the bishop of Rome is suggested for western Christendom by history, despite all its burdens. This connection to Rome must also be an object of dialogue with the Eastern churches. While their historical development has been oriented to other centers of Christendom, a primacy of honor for the bishop of Rome, in the sense of a "presider in love,"[72] is fundamentally possible for them.

4.6 Conclusions

(192) From the New Testament and the history of theology and the church, as well as on the basis of contemporary theological reflection, the following basic conditions arise for an agreement on the Petrine Ministry as a ministry for the unity of the universal church.

4.6.1 *For the Roman Catholic Side:*

(193) For unity in relation to the papal office, it is necessary but also sufficient, if a church can fundamentally recognize the following.

1. The office with universal responsibility in the church for the unity of believers in the truth of the gospel, as witnessed to in the figure of the apostle Peter in different strands of the New Testament, belongs to the essential and therefore indelible structures of the church in the sense of a necessary service to the saving gospel.[73]

2. The core of this office is realized historically in the person and calling of the bishop of Rome, that is, the Roman pope.

3. To the core of this office belong all the functions and actions that are necessary to fulfill and ensure its task in the universal church. This includes above all the binding competence in leadership and teaching without which the office bearer could not effectively exercise the care entrusted to him for the unity of the church in the truth of the gospel.

4.6.2 *For the Lutheran Side:*

(194) According to Lutheran theology, the following can be said regarding a universal office of leadership:

1. There are no fundamental objections to a church-wide Petrine Ministry as a pastoral service to the worldwide communion of churches and their common witness to the truth.

2. This ministry must be closely bound to obligatory structures of collegial and synodical common responsibility and must allow the independence of regional particular churches, including their confessional character.

3. In questions of doctrine, the sovereignty of Holy Scripture, as well as the comprehensive responsibility of all the baptized, must be preserved.

4.6.3 *Together, Catholics and Lutherans can say:*

(195)   A universal ministry serving the unity and truth of the church corresponds to the essence and the task of the church, which is realized on the local, regional, and universal level. It is appropriate to the nature of the church. This ministry represents all of Christendom and has a pastoral duty to all particular churches.

(196)   This ministry is obligated to be true to the biblical word as well as to the binding tradition of the Church. It is necessarily bound to the structures in which the *communio* takes shape, which are defined by conciliarity, collegiality, and subsidiarity.

(197)   Such common insights allow considerable room for various approaches on detailed questions regarding theology, history, and church law, e.g., the question of whether the historical Jesus instituted the office of Peter, when and how such an office was developed, or how the functions of this office have come to the bishop of Rome. Questions of political, canonical, and historically conditioned form and concretization of the ministry of Peter can remain open.

(198)   Problems of agreement arise in relation to the declarations of Vatican I about the *primacy of jurisdiction* and the *infallibility* of the Pope:

- For a Lutheran understanding, the principle of a "primacy of jurisdiction" is unacceptable, unless its form is constitutionally embedded in the *communio* structure of the church. The principle of *infallibility* is also unacceptable for a Lutheran understanding unless *ex cathedra* decisions by the pope remain under the final proviso of the revelation given in Holy Scripture.

- The Catholic side recognizes the justification for these considerations. It affirms that also in Catholic teaching, primacy of jurisdiction has its place only within the *communio* structure of the church.[74] In addition, it is convinced that papal infallibility can be exercised solely in absolute loyalty to the apostolic faith *(Holy Scripture)*[75] so that a pope who does not maintain this loyalty has by that fact forfeited his office.

- Both sides would welcome an official interpretation along such lines.

(199)   A reconciliation in relation to the Petrine Ministry can only be thought of as change and conversion, as a new beginning of universal communion on the basis of the common traditions that define us. This task faces all churches equally. Church-wide unity would include mutual recognition as churches, agreement in the understanding of the apostolic faith, communion in the sacraments and mutual recognition of the ministries to which word and sacrament are entrusted. This unity is oriented to the participation of all churches throughout Christendom. In this context, one must ask whether and to what degree the historical form of the papal office has preserved the true, enduring, and indispensable heart of the Petrine Ministry.

(200)   One must further pose the question of whether and to what degree the Roman Catholic Church fundamentally sees a possibility of a form of communion of the non-Catholic churches with the pope, in which the essence of the Petrine Ministry of unity is preserved, but in canonical forms other than those that have been presented as normative since the Middle Ages, and especially in the modern period. Starting points for the pursuit of this conversation might be:

- The possibility of an orientation to the exercise of primacy in the first Christian millennium without reference to later developments.

- A differentiation among the offices united in the person of the pope: bishop of Rome, pastor of the whole Church, head of the College of Bishops, patriarch of the West, primate of Italy, archbishop and metropolitan of the church province of Rome, sovereign of Vatican City.

- The shape of the Church as a *communio* of sister churches.[76]

- The development of the relationship between the church of Rome and the Catholic Eastern Catholic churches that are united with it.

- The legitimate variety in liturgy, theology, spirituality, leadership, and praxis.

Notes

[1] Cf. LG, 40.1.

[2] *The Lutheran Understanding of Ministry*, LWF Studies (Geneva 1983) par. 2.

[3] *Evangelischer Erwachsenenkatechismus* (Gütersloh: Gerd Mohn, 1975) par. 1161.

[4] LG, 10–12; AA, 3.

[5] *Gotteslob*, no. 48.3.

[6] *The Ministry in the Church*, par. 13.

[7] Cf. KWS, par. 61.

[8] LG 32.

[9] LG, 32.

[10] LG, 32.

[11] *Evangelischer Erwachsenenkatechismus*, par. 1162.

[12] *The Ministry in the Church*, par. 15.

[13] LG, 10.

[14] Cf. *The Ministry in the Church*, par. 20, n. 23.

[15] *Catechism of the Catholic Church*, par. 1547.

[16] LG, 32; cf. Augustine, Sermon 340.1.

[17] KWS, par. 61.

[18] CA 14.

[19] CA 5.

[20] Response of the VELKD to *Condemnations of the Reformation Era*, Amt, l.c., in *Lehrverurteilungen im Gespräch* (Göttingen: Vandenhoeck & Ruprecht, 1993) 142.

[21] Report of the Committee on the Department on the Laity, *The New Delhi Report: The Third Assembly of the World Council of Churches* 1961 (London: SCM Press, 1962) 203.

[22] AA 7.

[23] *Luther's Works*, vol. 31 (Philadelphia: Fortress Press, 1957) 355; cf. WA 7, 28.

[24] AA, 10.

[25] Cf. *Church and Justification*, par. 205.

[26] *Church and Justification*, par. 80.

[27] *The Church: Local and Universal*. A Study Document Commissioned and Received by the Joint Working Group of the World Council of Churches and the Roman Catholic Church (1990), in *Growth in Agreement II*, 862–75.

[28] Cf. LG, 23, and *Code of Canon Law*, can. 368f.

[29] Cr. LG, 28; SC, 42; *The Church: Local and Universal*, par. 18.

[30] *Church and Justification*, pars. 91–95.

[31] Cf. above, esp. par. 143.

[32] *The Ministry in the Church*, par. 69.

[33] AAS 59 (1967) 498; also *Condemnations of the Reformation Era*, 157–159.

[34] John Paul II, *Ut unum sint*, pars. 88–97.

[35] In the Malta Report of 1972, par. 66 (*Growth in Agreement I*, 184); in *Ways to Community* of 1980 (*Growth in Agreement I*, 215ff.); in *The Ministry in the Church* of 1981, pars. 67–73

(*Growth in Agreement I*, 269–71); in *Facing Unity* of 1984, pars. 100ff. (*Growth in Agreement II*, 467); in *Church and Justification* of 1995, par. 106 (*Growth in Agreement II*, 511f.).

[36] KWS, pars. 74, 76.

[37] *Condemnations of the Reformation Era*, 157–59.

[38] See above, par. 145.

[39] Ignatius of Antioch, *Romans*, 3.1; 1 Clement.

[40] Gregory VII definitively claims this title in *Dictatus papae* (1075).

[41] Demonstrably since Innocent III (1198–1216).

[42] The investiture controversy, the *Dictatus Papae* of Gregory VII.

[43] DH 870–75; its final sentence (DH 875) states that it is absolutely necessary for salvation that every human creature be subject to the Roman pontiff. The Lutheran Confessions refer to this claim: *Treatise on the Power and Primacy of the Pope* (TPPP), 3, 36, in Kolb and Wengert, 330, 336.

[44] CIC, can. 1404; cf. also TPPP, par. 50.

[45] Cf. also TPPP, par. 38.

[46] Cf. DH 3069, 3112–117.

[47] Cf. LG, 25.

[48] Cf. above, par. 156.

[49] Cf. SA II, 4 (Kolb and Wengert, 307–10; TPPP, 3, 36.

[50] Cf. TPPP, 38ff.

[51] *Luther's Works*, vol. 26, 99 (WA 40 I,181).

[52] Cf. WA 6, 602, 605.

[53] SA, II, 4 (Kolb and Wengert, 309); TPPP, par. 39.

[54] SA II,4 (Kolb and Wengert, 307f.).

[55] Signature to the SA (Kolb and Wengert, 326).

[56] TPPP, pars. 7ff.

[57] TPPP, par. 16.

[58] WA 10 III, 208ff.

[59] TPPP, pars. 23f.

[60] TPPP, par. 31.

[61] Statement of the Protestant and Catholic Bishops of Thuringia and Saxony-Anhalt on the 450th Anniversary of the Death of Martin Luther, February 2, 1996.

[62] *Church and Justification*, par. 214.

[63] DV, 10.

[64] Cf. ch. IV, 1.6 and 1.8.

[65] Cf. KWS, par. 74 and the Resolution of the Church Leadership of the VELKD as well as their letter to the German Bishops' Conference; further, *Condemnations of the Reformation Era*, 158f, 185 as well as the Resolution of the VELKD/Arnoldshainer Konferenz on the 1994 official response to *Condemnations of the Reformation Era*, 4.1.4, *Texte aus der VELKD*, no. 42 (1996).

[66] Cf. the Lutheran-Roman Catholic dialogue in the U.S.A.

[67] CA 28; Apol. 28; TPPP 60ff.

[68] *The Ministry in the Church*, par. 45.

[69] *Church and Justification*, par. 117.

[70] Cf. par. 149.

[71] *Baptism, Eucharist and Ministry*, par. M26f.

[72] Ignatius, *To the Romans*.

[73] Cf. *Church and Justification*, par. 196. The distinction between elements necessary for the ministry of the church and elements necessary to the saving gospel is presented here in relation to the episcopate and apostolic succession.

[74] Cf. LG, 13.

[75] Cf. LG, 25.

[76] LG, 23.

Chapter 7

The Communion of Saints Beyond Death

1. Eternal Life in Full Communion with the Triune God

(201)   Just as the love of God gives itself to humanity in eternal faith-fulness, so also everything that is the consequence and form of this love will endure, including the calling to the communion of saints effected in baptism and through which the person gains "being in Christ" (cf. 1 Cor 12:12f.; 2 Cor 5:17). Therefore, the Christian bears the faith convic-tion that death is not the end of the "communion of saints"; it extends beyond this age.

(202)   The third article of the Apostles' Creed speaks of the commun-ion of saints and says: "I believe in . . . the resurrection of the dead (lit-erally: 'of the flesh') and the life everlasting." The Nicene Creed also expresses our common hope: "We look for the resurrection of the dead, and the life of the world to come." Thus the Christian confession con-tradicts today's widely held dictum that everything ends with death. Conversely, Christian hope contradicts a belief in reincarnation, which anticipates a purification of human life as a result of multiple reembodi-ments and which awaits its final fulfillment in a nameless transition into an empty infinity.

(203)   In many New Testament passages "eternal life" describes life in the "age to come" (e.g., Mark 10:30 par). Believers already have a share in this life (compare John 3:36) because they receive the Spirit of God as "guarantee" and "first fruits" (Rom 8:23; 2 Cor 1:22; 5:5; Eph 1:14). "If

the Spirit of him who raised Jesus from the dead dwells in you, he who raised Christ from the dead will give life to your mortal bodies also through his Spirit that dwells in you" (Rom 8:11).

(204)   None of our concepts are sufficient to describe "eternal life." As life in a new eon, it goes beyond our earthly experience. "Eternity" does not simply mean "limitless duration" but the fulfillment of our transitory life in the participation in the life of the Triune God. "He only who gives true happiness gives eternal life, that is, an endlessly happy life."[1]

(205)   The Christian message gains the content of its understanding of "eternal life" from the revelation of this life in Jesus Christ (1 John 1:2). In him, "eternal life" has appeared in earthly reality and become open to our experience. In its ultimacy, however, eternal life remains withdrawn from our powers of imagination: "We are God's children now; what we will be has not yet been fulfilled" (1 John 3:2). Because we will be like him, we hope that "we will see him as he is" (ibid). The Christian tradition speaks of a "beatific vision of God" and of the "eternal light," which shines on those who come to complete communion with Christ.

(206)   Against Platonic and Gnostic currents in early Christianity, which simply assumed an immortality of the soul, early church theology emphatically professed faith in the resurrection of the flesh and thereby in a personal identity in a new physicality beyond death.

(207)   In the language of the Old Testament, "flesh" describes humans in their creatureliness, in their fallenness, and at the same time in their interweaving with all humanity and the whole of creation (cf. Gen 7:21). The promise of the vision of the glory of the Lord applies to "all flesh" (Isa 40:5). The Christian "praise of the flesh"[2] is grounded in the Son of God taking on flesh, and, risen from the dead, carrying this human flesh into the life of God, giving us his flesh as food (John 6:53-56) as the basis of the promise of eternal life with him and resurrection on the last day. It is true of his flesh also that it does not in and of itself survive death, but that God's Spirit creates new life (John 6:63; 1 Pet 3:18). The Risen One gives himself to be recognized by his own through the fleshly signs of his passion (John 20:20, 27; cf. Rev 5:6).

(208)   *Paul* speaks of a transformation (1 Cor 15:51) of our earthly-bodily existence into a "spiritual" body (1 Cor 15:44) through the resurrection

of the dead. This transformation means that there is something lasting, our personal identity, and, through this new creation, also something new that eludes our imagination. Paul applies the analogy of the relation of the seed to that which grows out of it after it dies (1 Cor 15:35-38). "Resurrection of the flesh" means not the resuscitation of dead bodies, but a new embodiment of human persons, in which their personal identities shaped by their histories are raised by God and made complete in communion with the resurrected Christ.

(209)   Like the Holy Scriptures, the entire *tradition* of the church affirms that the human "I" continues beyond death. This conviction is very often expressed by the concept "soul" (Matt 10:28). This concept does not restrict us to a particular anthropology. That death is not the last word is also thoroughly consistent with anthropological insights of our time. We agree that humans are "souls" and continue beyond death because they were created by God's Spirit and stand before his countenance: "You created us for yourself, and our heart is restless until it rests in you."[3]

(210)   In order to resist the picture of a, so to speak, natural immortality, many recent Protestant theologians consciously have avoided the concept "soul." They want to underline that death radically affects the whole person and that the resurrection of the dead is completely a deed of God. This concern to take death truly seriously is also increasingly strong in contemporary Catholic theology. On the other hand, Protestant theologians also increasingly emphasize the continuity, which Paul expresses when he speaks of the deceased as "those who have fallen asleep" in Christ (cf. 1 Cor 15:18, 51; 1 Thess 4:14) and of their "being changed." Together we can say today that the transition from death to life is a creative act of God.

(211)   The life to which we are already born anew (cf. John 3:5) on earth through the Spirit of God reaches beyond physical death. This life whose history ends with bodily death is raised by God in a fulfillment that is not worth comparing with the "sufferings of the present time" (Rom 8:18), in which every yearning of the human being also finds a fulfillment that infinitely transcends that yearning. "Blessed are the dead, who from now on die in the Lord. 'Yes,' says the Spirit, 'they will rest from their labors, for their deeds will follow them'" (Rev 14:13). Their names (cf. Rev 3:5; Phil 4:3) and their works (Rev 20:12) will be

written in the "book of life." Having come through the great ordeal, they have "washed their robes and made them white in the blood of the Lamb" (Rev 7:14), and "God will wipe away every tear from their eyes" (Rev 7:17).

(212)   In both creeds, the concept "resurrection" connects the fate of the dead with the statement of faith that Jesus Christ is "resurrected" and sits on the right hand of God. Only by the "resurrection of the flesh" and "eternal life" do humans partake "in Christ": "for as all die in Adam, so all will be made alive in Christ" (1 Cor 1:22). Resurrection to eternal life only takes place in communion with Christ, which includes becoming like him in a death like his (Rom 6:5). This happens through baptism in a life shaped by baptism.

Inevitably every person, even those who are in Christ, must die in the sense that they experience their own death as the end of all earthly possibilities of life, for "it is appointed for mortals to die once, and after that the judgment" (Heb 9:27). The Apostles' Creed says of the Son of God: He "descended to the dead." It is thereby expressed that he suffered human death to its greatest depths (cf. Matt 12:40; 26:37-39; 27:46).

That the Son of God descended to the dead implies also that "having fallen asleep for a short time, he raises those from the kingdom of the dead."[4] To the communion of eternal life in Christ belong therefore, "as is read in the Fathers, all the just, from Adam on, and from Abel, the just one, to the last of the elect."[5]

(213)   In the inevitable encounter with Christ "each of us will be accountable to God" (Rom 14:12). "For all of us must appear before the judgment seat of Christ, so that each may receive recompense for what has been done in the body, whether good or evil" (2 Cor 5:10). Here is decided for each individual whether they will receive the "eternal life" for which they were originally meant (cf. 1 Tim 6:12; 2 Pet 1:10). In this "judgment," however, not only will the good and bad deeds of humanity be revealed, but above all and finally "the goodness and loving-kindness of God our Savior," who justifies us not on the basis of our works, but "according to his mercy" (Titus 3:4f.).

(214)   As certain as we may be of the justifying and saving mercy of God, we have no right and occasion for security: Jesus warns repeatedly and vividly of the danger of missing the mark. With human freedom comes also the possibility of human error, so that we must reckon

with the possibility of eternal ruin. Paul admonishes, "work out your own salvation with fear and trembling" (Phil 2:12). Jesus answers the curious question, how many "will be saved," with the admonition to the questioner: "Strive to enter through the narrow door" (Luke 13:24).

(215)   It is not for us to judge those who according to human judgment do not believe or refuse to repent. Nevertheless, we can prayerfully entrust them to the mercy of God (Rom 11:32), whose love for the world is so great that he "gave his only Son" to save the world and all humanity (John 3:16f.; Titus 2:11).

(216)   In Holy Scripture and in both creeds of the early church, the judgment of the living and the dead is bound up with the (Second) Coming in glory of the Son of God, Jesus Christ. At the same time it is witnessed in the Scriptures that those who believe are with Christ immediately after death (Luke 23:43; Phil 1:23). How personal and universal fulfillment relate to one another is not reflected in the Bible. Later theological tradition distinguished here between particular and universal judgment.

(217)   In reflection on the relationship of time and eternity, Protestant and Catholic theologians alike support the belief that personal and universal fulfillment must be regarded as a differentiated unity, in consciousness of the limits of the eschatological powers of imagination. The distinction between a "particular" or "personal" judgment and "the manifestation of the glory of our great God and Savior, Jesus Christ" (Titus 2:13) must not be misunderstood as a separation.

(218)   The Nicene Creed says, "his kingdom will have no end." Kingdom *(basilea)* here describes the kingdom and reign of Christ (cf. Luke 23:42; Eph 5:5; Col 1:13; 2 Pet 1:11). According to the will of God the whole cosmos, all "things in heaven and things on earth" (Eph 1:10), should find its fulfillment when Christ "hands over the kingdom to God the Father" (1 Cor 15:24). The Son of God is not only "the firstborn of the dead," but also "the firstborn of all creation": "in him all things in heaven and on earth were created, things visible and invisible . . . all things have been created through him and for him" (Col 1:15ff.).

(219)   The Holy Scriptures are also acquainted with metaphors which portray a living, eschatological communion with Christ, e.g., the wed-

ding banquet (Rev 19:9) and the "new Jerusalem" (Rev 21:2–22:5). Like the "body of Christ," these images express a sense of being with one another that is also constituted as an all-embracing being for one another. Any merely individualistic understanding of "eternal life" is not in keeping with the Christian message. Thus it is the task of the church on earth to pray and work that "the entire world may enter the people of God, the body of the Lord and the temple of the Holy Spirit, and that in Christ, the head of all, all honor and glory may be rendered to the Creator and Father of the Universe."[6]

(220)   The church celebrates its deepest mystery as the communion of saints centrally in the Eucharist, in which it "proclaims the Lord's death until he comes" (1 Cor 11:26). The eschatological meaning of the Eucharist is emphasized in The Gospel of John: "Those who eat my flesh and drink my blood have eternal life, and I will raise them up on the last day" (John 6:54). The Letter to the Hebrews, with its stronger metaphorical language oriented towards the Old Testament temple cult, suggests that in the church as the New Testament community of salvation on earth, the eschatological community of saints is already present in this age and is celebrated in the worship of the church: "You have come to Mount Zion and to the city of the living God, the heavenly Jerusalem, and to innumerable angels in festal gathering, and to the assembly of the firstborn who are enrolled in heaven" (Heb 12:22f.). Similar images are found in the scenes of the heavenly liturgy in The Revelation of John. When the church sings in its liturgy, "Holy, holy, holy Lord, God of power and might. Heaven and earth are full of your glory," it thereby then joins on earth in the thankful praise of every angel and saint in heaven. The church knows it is united with them in thanksgiving for the life that comes from God, and in that life it experiences its fulfillment.

(221)   The calling to give testimony today to the new life in the communion of saints belongs essentially to every member of the church: "Always be ready to make your defense to anyone who demands from you an accounting for the hope that is in you" (1 Pet 3:15). The Nicene Creed expresses that Christian hope with the "expectation" of the resurrection of the dead and the life of the world to come. This hope leaves its characteristic stamp on the Christian life in this world oriented towards the gospel (cf. Acts 23:6; Rom 5:2; 1 Cor 15:19; 1 Thess 4:13f.; 1 Pet 1:3). Death and destruction have lost their finality for those who are already born anew and raised to new life through the Spirit.

(222) The kingdom of God alone is final, and it is "righteousness, peace, and joy in the Holy Spirit" (Rom 14:17). Shaped by these gifts of its Lord, the church is on the way to its fulfillment in the kingdom of God. "Until there shall be new heavens and a new earth in which justice dwells (cf. 2 Pet 3:13) the pilgrim Church in her sacraments and institutions, which pertain to this present time, has the appearance of this world which is passing and she herself dwells among creatures who groan and travail in pain until now and await the revelation of the sons of God (cf. Rom 8:19-22)."[7] The vision of the new Jerusalem (Rev 21:1ff.), the new creation for God's people, in which the tree of life stands, portrays the names of the twelve tribes of the sons of Israel on the gates of the city and the names of the twelve apostles of the Lamb on its cornerstones, the signature of the history of God's people in this age.

2. Prayer for the Dead

(223) Together we are convinced that it corresponds to the communion in which we are bound together in Christ beyond death with those who have already died to pray for them and to commend them in loving memory to the mercy of God.[8] All people—including those who have led a Christian life—remain sinners who fall short of God's demand and have need for the accepting love of the merciful God.

(224) In this context the question is raised whether this acceptance in the mercy of God is to be understood as a process of a purification of the dead. Catholic teaching speaks here of a *purgatorium* (purification, purgatory). This concept says in essence that the dead become cognizant of their sinfulness in its profoundest depths before the face of God and experience as a burning anguish their own lovelessness when faced with God's love. Thereby they will be cleansed "as through fire" (1 Cor 3:15) by means of the infinite love of God that embraces and heals them. In this, according to Catholic thought, the intercessory prayer of those still living can be of help.

(225) In the history of piety, spatial and temporal conceptions have attached themselves to the doctrine of purgatory. Misunderstandings and abuses have often eclipsed the authentic fundamental idea. The practices of indulgences also contributed to this. The Council of Trent enjoined the bishops that "uncertain things, or things which labor under an appearance of error, should not be made public and treated of. Those

things which tend to a certain curiosity or superstition, or which savor of shameful profit, let them prohibit as scandals and stumbling-blocks to the faithful."[9]

(226)   In particular, it was ecclesiastical practice connected at the time to the idea of "purgatory" that sparked the protest of the Reformation. The consensus that has been reached in the meantime on the message of justification will thus have to prove itself exactly on this point.

(227)   Against the idea of a temporal process of purification after death, Protestant theology has always maintained that the human being's pilgrim status *(status viatoris)* definitively ends at death. That is also a Catholic conviction. Our prayer for the dead in the communion of Christ still remains meaningful, however, because before God it is not bound to our conceptions of time.

(228)   Today we can speak together of a purification in the following sense: the communion in Christ into which human beings are called endures also in death and judgment. It becomes complete as, through the pain over failure in earthly life, persons come with their love to give the perfect response to the love of God. That this may take place, the communion of the faithful on earth may constantly pray on the basis of the all-sufficient sacrifice of Christ. This prayer is, like the veneration of the saints, a liturgical expression of their eschatological hope.

3. The Veneration of the Saints

(229)   The saints comprise "a great multitude that no one can count, from every nation, from all peoples and languages" (Rev 7:9). At the same time, some persons from this multitude have left their mark on the memory of the church in special ways, persons who have lived and died as exemplary disciples of Christ in the community of faith of their time. To this group belong, first of all, those who have spilled their blood in witness to the faith *(martyrs)* and also later ascetics and confessors. Saints in this sense are those members of the church who solely by grace and faith have lived out love and other Christian virtues in an exemplary fashion and whose witness has found recognition in the church after their death. They all comprise the "cloud of witnesses" (Heb 12:1) with whom the communion of saints on earth has a permanent union.

(230)   The Roman Catholic and Lutheran Churches agree "that one should honor the saints."[10] They understand such honor to encompass thanks to God who has called people to holiness, faith in the power of his grace, more powerful than sin, and confession of his goodness in which he calls forth in history fellow human beings as living examples of the Christian life.

(231)   In the debates of the sixteenth century, controversy flamed over whether "a person should invoke the saints or seek help from them." The Reformers rejected this because they saw Christ's role as the sole mediator being threatened.[11] Luther designates the "invocation of the saints" as "one of the abuses of the Antichrist."[12]

The Council of Trent wanted to protect the conviction of Catholic tradition and declared that the cult of the saints was legitimate and in accordance with the Scriptures. It was not, however, decreed as mandatory but recommended as appropriate.[13] In addition, the council accepted the criticism of the Reformers by urging the bishops to resist actual widespread abuses and on the whole to supervise the cult.[14] Current Catholic canon law states: "Veneration through public cult is permitted only to those servants of God who are listed in the catalog of the saints or of the blessed by the authority of the Church."[15] On the other hand, the presupposition for the canonization of saints and blessed dead is that they already enjoy a certain honor among Christian people.

(232)   The historic debates have determined confessional stances up to the present day. These positions embody concerns that have lasting meaning for both sides: the biblical teaching of Christ's role as the sole mediator and justification by faith alone, insight into the constant threat of abuses and the defense against them, maintenance of the confession that death forms no boundary for the communion of saints and "that the saints are to be remembered so that we may strengthen our faith when we see how they experienced grace and how they were helped by faith."[16] In view of these facts, we should attempt to achieve a better understanding of the universal communion of saints, on the basis of Holy Scripture and of our common faith tradition.

(233)   The new reflection on the ecclesiological meaning of the saints undertaken at the Second Vatican Council contributes to this attempt on the Catholic side.[17] On the Lutheran side, the fact is again taken seriously that from the Reformation to the present day the saints have had

their durable place in the liturgy and hymnal. Lutheran worship books since the Reformation have contained schedules for days set aside to commemorate the saints. In current liturgies and lectionaries there are orders and texts for days to commemorate the individual apostles and evangelists, martyrs, teachers of the church, All Saints, and for the biblically attested Marian days (Presentation of the Lord in the Temple— "Candlemass," Annunciation to Mary, and the Visitation), which are understood as festivals of Christ. In the hymnal the saints are lifted up above all in the hymns on the church and on eternal life. The names of individual saints are rarely mentioned; more frequent are references to the communion of the sanctified as a whole or to apostles, prophets, patriarchs, etc.[18]

(234) Together we can testify: "In the earthly liturgy, . . . we sing a hymn to the Lord's glory with all the warriors of the heavenly army; venerating the memory of the saints, we hope for some part and fellowship with them; we eagerly await the Saviour, Our Lord Jesus Christ, until He, our life, shall appear and we too will appear with him in glory."[19]

(235) The entire existence of the saints is given shape into its very roots and brought to maturity through the grace of Christ. Without this grace the saints have no significance for the church, but by it they become witnesses of the love of God for humanity. Therefore they became helpful models for our faith. Because their lives took shape, not from their own accomplishments, but as disciples of Christ, their honor is always and above all oriented to the honor of the one they followed. The praise of the saints is the praise of the goodness of the Triune God, who has revealed himself through his Son, the only mediator between God and humanity.

(236) When the faithful worship God, they honor God also in all his works. To these works belong the communion of saints as a work of his grace. It is realized in those who stand in the circle of Christ's disciples and who accordingly live out the gifts given to them. Thus all Christians deserve to be honored, especially those who have lived out their Christian existence in an exemplary manner unto death.

(237) According to *Catholic tradition* venerating God and venerating the saints are connected to each other and at the same time are carefully distinguished from one another. This is maintained in the following

theological concepts: God alone is the object of our worship *(latria, ado-ratio)*; the saints deserve veneration *(dulia, veneratio).*[20]

(238)   Also the *Lutheran tradition,* which honors the exemplary witness of faith of the saints, sees a connection between the remembrance of the saints and the worship of God. As much as it emphasizes that the Tri-une God alone is to be called upon in prayer, the remembrance of the saints still has its place in prayer: in thanksgiving and intercession the church remembers the gracious work of God that has taken shape in the life and prayer of the saints and abides eternally.

(239)   From these considerations a path has opened towards an agree-ment on previously contentious questions about the intercession of the saints and the possibility of their invocation.

(240)   The saints are holy as justified persons who lead lives of faith and love. They are a living interpretation of the message of the gospel. In them God's salvation is made concrete both humanly and histori-cally. They are thus witnesses of Christ in that the Lord meets us in them, for the church is his body: Just as all life currents proceed from Christ into all his members, so all spiritual connections among the members are mediated through him. Therefore when one member suf-fers, all suffer, and when one member rejoices, all rejoice (1 Cor 12:26f.). Christians thus remain forever bound to one another, even beyond the dividing line of death. With Origen one may confess that the saints in heaven intercede for us in fulfillment of their love for their neighbor.[21]

(241)   Catholic tradition draws the conclusion that it is possible to ask the saints for this prayer. The reservation of every prayer made in the Spirit of Christ applies here: that the will of God be fulfilled in all things. Invocation and intercession of the saints neither circumvent nor dimin-ish Christ's role as the sole mediator; rather, only because of him are such conceivable and possible for the faithful.

(242)   The Reformers also have not rejected in principle the interces-sion of the dead. The *Apology of the Augsburg Confession* grants that not only angels but also the saints in heaven pray for the church.[22] Never-theless, they may never be declared as reconcilers and thereby as media-tors of salvation, as if they were more accessible and more reconciling than the Savior himself.

(243)   Together we bear witness to the communion of saints that in the risen Christ includes both the living and the dead (Rom 14:7-9). In the manner in which we express this communion in worship services and in personal spiritual lives, differences exist between our churches. According to Lutheran understanding, the remembrance of the saints occurs solely in our praying to God. In the Catholic church, the remembrance of the saints can take the form of an invocation, which is made possible only in Christ and is to be distinguished from praying to Christ. Insofar as these conditions in doctrine and practice are maintained and Christ's role as the sole mediator is not diminished, this difference, according to Lutheran thinking, is not church dividing.

(244)   When the veneration of the saints is seen along with its christological, soteriological, and ecclesiological premises and conditions, it need no longer be church dividing. This presupposes, however, that both sides attempt to take seriously the theological grounding and to draw consequences from it. For one side, this means the avoidance of everything that can lead to misinterpretations and abuses concerning the veneration of the saints. For the other, it means to keep in mind the intention of the veneration of the saints and to make some effort toward understanding the concrete and traditional forms of this cult.

(245)   The veneration of the saints is a form of love. Love is a stirring of the heart. The form of its expression cannot be measured with the standard of an all too sober rationalism, although it must also be theologically responsible. The veneration of the saints shows all forms and manners of human, concrete love and is therefore always bound by time and culture. It is realized in the churches in very different ways. Therefore, its form can neither be binding for all Christians nor be called into question in principle by other particular traditions.

(246)   The veneration of the saints is above all a form of venerating God. When Christians venerate any *one* saint, they turn to God and in God to *all* saints. In Catholic thought it is likewise humanly reasonable to grant certain sainted persons a special relationship to particular dimensions of our world. Individual saints have never manifested all aspects of the Christian life, but certain specific ones in exemplary fashion. Whoever dies in the Lord, their deeds follow them (cf. Rev 14:13); and they will be "pillars in the temple of my God" (Rev 3:12). Therefore, Christians have occasionally emphasized specific relationships

between a saint and one sector of reality: saints became patrons of houses of God and communities, vocations, offices, etc. *(patrocinium)*. This should encourage Christians to make good use of their gifts of grace for the edification of the church. In this context belongs the old custom of giving the name of a saint at baptism: the new bearers of this name should feel a bond with this saint as their example. In the Catholic liturgy of the Easter Vigil, the patron saints of that congregation and place, as well as the names of the baptized, can be inserted into the litany for all the saints.

(247)   It is also familiar to Lutheran thought to name church buildings and church institutions after witnesses of the faith. As a rule the names of the medieval church buildings were retained, and new churches were named after generally recognized saints or witnesses to Christian faith and love from post-Reformation times. They point to the interconnection of the church within history and at the same time serve as models for specific congregations or church groups. The "Lutheran Calendar of Commemorations"[23] assigns each day to individual saints. Descriptions of their lives underline their significance. In many Lutheran houses of worship there are older and more recent art works that depict saints.

(248)   *Pilgrimages* are a further form of devotion to the saints. These are particularly widespread in the Catholic Church. They have their basis in the knowledge that the Christian life itself is a pilgrimage, but also in the ancient human experience of the nearness of God at certain places. This experience makes contact with the fact that God himself appeared in Jesus Christ among us human beings at a specific place and at a specific time. Therefore, it is understandable when people journey to a place where others before them have had concrete faith experiences. With St. Augustine we can say: "God is, of course, everywhere, and he who created all things is not contained or enclosed by any place, and he must be adored by his true adorers in spirit and in truth, in order that, hearing in secret, he may also justify and crown them in secret. With regard, nonetheless, to those actions of God that are visibly know to human beings, who can search out his plan as to why these miracles occur in some places and do not occur in others?"[24]

(249)   Lutheran Christians also know of setting out for other places where they have access to fellowship with other believers and look forward to renewal in their personal faith. Thus there are journeys to places

like Taizé, to the Luther sites, or to places which are connected with recognized witnesses of faith. Just as in the Catholic church, pilgrimages to the Holy Land are treasured in the Lutheran church. Lutherans usually do not, however, go on pilgrimages to places that are marked by the saints and their veneration. Here is felt still the effect of the abuses that were objected to in the pilgrimages of the late Middle Ages; this objection came not only from the Reformers but from Catholic Christians as well.[25]

(250)   The *veneration of relics* is to be seen as one form of honoring the saints. It goes back to the period of the early church. The foundational thought is the faithfulness of God which affirms the whole human being, thus also their physical bodies. According to its inmost intentions, the veneration of the remains of sainted persons confesses that the whole of history, even that of the individual, is saved by God. The veneration of relics was nurtured mostly in the Middle Ages; the boundaries of a healthy piety were not seldom overstepped.

(251)   In the *Catholic* world the cult of relics still has its place today. It finds its expression in the custom of displaying a "reliquary" inside every altar. By this the faith witness of the martyrs is connected to the living witness of the congregation that celebrates the Eucharist (Rev 6:9).

(252)   The loving preservation of signs of remembrance of people we honor is also found in the *Lutheran* world. There is no objection to this, insofar as the memorials honoring them lead to thanksgiving to God. But where a mediation of grace is expected from the veneration of relics, a shared protest will still arise today.

4. The Veneration of Mary, the Mother of the Lord

(253)   Since New Testament times, Mary has taken a special place among the "cloud of witnesses." By God's own gracious care alone, she was selected to become the mother of Jesus Christ; in exemplary faith she accepted this calling (Luke 1:26-56). All her life she remains a hearer of the Word of God and contemplates in her heart the events of her son's life up to the cross. After his resurrection, she awaited the coming of the Holy Spirit upon God's people, "constantly devoting [herself] to prayer, together with . . . [Jesus'] brothers" (Acts 1:14). In all this she embodies the calling and destiny of the disciples of the Lord and becomes the

representative of the new covenant people. This comes to expression partly in the designation given her already in the early church and often used of her today: "sister in the faith." She is "image and beginning of the church as it is to be perfected is the world to come," and she "shines forth on earth, until the day of the Lord shall come (cf. 2 Pet 3:10), as a sign of sure hope and solace to the people of God during its sojourn on earth."[26] Thus she has—just like all other Christians and at the same time in a special way because of her special salvation-historical task— an unmistakable place in the communion of saints: the task which God intended for her and gave to her, to be the mother of his Son, sets her apart from all people and gives her a special significance.

(254)   In the history of the church, the New Testament beginnings have been developed in varying ways and with differing precision. Already in the ancient church it proved theologically necessary to confess Mary as the God-bearer and Virgin, in order precisely to express faith in Jesus Christ as true God and true man. That in turn prompted the devotion of Christians in liturgy and piety. If Mary, with salvation-historical consistency, has her place in the mysteries of incarnation and redemption, then her veneration is always and above all also veneration of these mysteries.

(255)   These interrelations were taught also in the Reformation and the subsequent Lutheran tradition. With the ancient Christian confession of faith, the Reformers explicitly accepted the ancient church's belief in Mary as the Mother of God and in her virginity.[27] Because she is the Mother of God it follows, as Luther said, that she is to be given "all honor, all blessedness, and her unique place in the whole of mankind, among which she has no equal, namely, that she had a child by the Father in heaven, and such a Child."[28]

(256)   Of course, the theological foundations of Marian devotion have not always and everywhere been attended to, nor have they always been clear in the particular forms of Marian devotion, especially in popular piety. In the course of time, exaggerations repeatedly arose in content or in form, leading to doctrinal distortion. On the one hand, there has been a "small-mindedness which obscures the figure and mission of Mary." On the other hand, there has been a "vain credulity, which substitutes reliance on merely external practices for serious commitment; . . . an ephemeral sentimentality, so alien to the spirit of the

Gospel that demands persevering and practical action."[29] That applies especially to the form of late medieval Marian piety encountered by the Reformers. They emphatically protested against that piety, and rightly so, as we today are together able to see. In post-Reformation times, this criticism led to Mary becoming a sign of confessional division.

(257)   Questionable for Lutheran Christians is not only Marian piety but also the Catholic development of Marian doctrine. Above all, offense was caused by the definition of the dogmas of Mary's Immaculate Conception (1854) and her Assumption into Heaven (1950). Neither statement has any direct anchoring in Holy Scripture.

(258)   The conflict thus created has appeared to this day so insurmountable that the doctrine and veneration of Mary has previously scarcely been a subject of ecumenical dialogue. In recent years a change has occurred in both churches. This is indicated in the emphasized sentence of the "Lutheran Adult Catechism": "Mary belongs to the gospel. Mary is not only 'Catholic'; she is also 'Lutheran.'"[30]

(259)   For *Catholic* thought, the so-called "new" Marian dogmas have come into being out of the meditative contemplation of the church over the centuries. It provides an answer to the question: "How is God at work in the life of a person whom he has chosen in such a unique way to be the mother of his Son?" The proposition of *the immaculate conception of Mary* is based in the believing knowledge of the faithfulness of God, who works all things "together for good for those who . . . are called according to his purpose" (Rom 8:28). It asserts that, from the moment of her conception by her parents, the mother of Jesus was freed from that guilt in which all people stand. For her, however, as for all people, Jesus' word still applies: "Apart from me you can do nothing" (John 15:5). She also has been redeemed by the justifying grace of God in Christ. In view of his coming redemptive death, however, this occurred already in the first moment of her existence, whereas for the rest of humanity it occurs later (for Christians in baptism). The dogma thus illustrates the power of the grace of God, who in sovereign freedom calls whom he wills and how he wills. It is at the same time a promise that God wills to draw us totally into his favor.

(260)   The statement of the *Assumption of Mary into Heaven* has its roots in the already cited reflection from the Letter to the Romans:

"Those whom he (i.e., God) justified he also glorified" (Rom 8:30). That means: when God once promises his election and grace to persons, and when they accept in faith that grace and live accordingly, then God grants them wholly (body and soul) blessed communion with him (heaven). What we confess in the last sentence of the Creed as a hope for us, this dogma confesses about the mother of the Lord in the past tense: she has reached what we are still moving toward—the resurrection of the dead and the life everlasting as fruit of the justifying favor of God.

(261)   *Lutheran* Christians can also believe that, already at the beginning of her earthly existence, God had determined that Mary would be an instrument of grace, as he had done also with Jeremiah (Jer 1:5) and John the Baptist (Luke 1:13-17). They must clearly disagree with the dogma of the Immaculate Conception if it were to propose that Mary was unbound from humanity caught in sin and placed on the same level as the sinless Christ. For "there is no distinction: since all have sinned and fall short of the glory of God; they are now justified by his grace as a gift, through the redemption that is in Christ Jesus" (Rom 3:22-24). As one redeemed by the death and resurrection of her son, Mary belongs to the communion of believers and does not stand above it. That applies also to her *Bodily Assumption into Heaven.* Lutheran Christians do not need to contradict the 1950 dogma, if it applies to Mary the hope expressed by Paul (Phil 1:23), that after her death she would be allowed to go home to her Redeemer. That is also our hope for ourselves and for all who have gone before us in faith. The Lutheran Church would of course see its faith in the one mediator Jesus Christ threatened if Mary were lifted out from the communion of believers and placed by the side of her Son as a sort of mediator.

(262)   The Second Vatican Council, the post-conciliar reordering of the liturgy, as well as several clarifying statements by the Catholic *magisterium,* and many theologians have given a renewed impetus to the Catholic interpretation of the Mother of Christ on the basis of the sources of the faith.[31] There is thus an opportunity today, on the basis of an unbiased and open consideration of history, to gain an understanding of the difficulties the topic of Mary offers for ecumenical discussion. It can also be made clear anew that this topic should be freshly taken up and discussed for the sake of the full proclamation of the word of God from the Scriptures.

(263) Sound reasons remain, now as before, which make Mary appear as a figure *between* the churches. These reasons are not always theological in nature, but—in spite of all clarifications—very often anchored in the area of emotions and confessional traditions. If a convergence is to be achieved, both Catholics and Lutherans need to show respect and understanding for the motives, concerns, and historical conditioning of the other. They must also summon the courage and freedom from prejudice to overcome all those barriers that do not need, for the sake of the faith, to remain in place.

(264) On the way toward this goal, it will be helpful if Catholics can make their own the concern of the Reformation that the role of Christ as the one Mediator, the primacy of faith and grace, and the preeminence of the word of God in the Bible are preserved precisely in relation to Mary. That will further theological conscientiousness in Mariology and a sober thoughtfulness in the veneration of Mary.

(265) As far as *Marian theology* is concerned, it should be kept in mind that the dogmas of the Immaculate Conception and the Assumption of Mary into Heaven, problematic for Reformation theology, differ from older Marian dogmas in that they are first of all not meant to defend the faith, but rather are meant to serve the praise of God. That does not mean that they are lacking in material content, but rather that they point in a deeply doxological direction: they are offered in praise of the pure grace of God. It may thus be asked whether it is necessary for the unity of the faith that Reformation theology makes these Marian dogmas its own if it is prepared to recognize that these statements are fundamentally in harmony with revelation.

(266) *Veneration of Mary* requires constant orientation to Christ. Consistent with the directives of Pope Paul VI, the veneration of Mary must be biblically grounded, liturgically oriented, consistent with contemporary anthropology, and ecumenically shaped.[32]

(267) Lutheran Christians should, for the sake of the same goal of the unity of the faith, honor the efforts of the Catholic side to establish the place of Mary christologically and ecclesiologically. They are invited to consider that for Catholic thought the Mother of Christ is the embodiment of the event of justification by grace alone and through faith. It is from that conception that the Marian dogmas of the nineteenth and twentieth

centuries are derived: If God elects a person in such a way as Mary, then Christian thought realizes that such a calling seizes that person totally—it begins in the first moment of that person's existence and never abandons that person. As far as the invocation and veneration of the Mother of God is concerned, there are no other rules or standards than those that are prescribed for all the saints. For Mary belongs, albeit as the most distinguished member, completely and fully in their communion.

(268)   For these reasons, however, Christians in the communion of saints who still find themselves on the pilgrimage of faith cannot forget the Mother of Christ. For "she sees that God alone is great in all things . . . She sees God in all things, depends on no creature, relates all things to God."[33] Our faith looks in the same direction.

Notes

[1] Augustine, *City of God* 6.12: CSEL 40/I,299.

[2] Tertullian, *De carnis resurrectione* 11: CSEL 47,39.

[3] Augustine, *Confessions* 1.1: PL 32.661.

[4] Attributed to Epiphanius, *Homilia in sancto et magno Sabbato*, PG 43, 440; cf. Matt 27:52; 1 Pet 3:18f.; 4:6.

[5] LG 2 with the passages quoted there.

[6] LG 17.

[7] LG 48.

[8] *In the Catholic Missal:* "We pray for our deceased *sister/brother:* We pray that *he/she,* purified from sin, may rise to the fullness of life. Give *him/her* a portion in the inheritance of your saints in light" (1130). "Cleanse *her/him* in the sight of Christ from *her/his* sins and lead *her/him* mercifully to final fulfillment" (1332). "Purify *her/him* through the Easter mystery of Christ and let *her/him* be raised to eternal joy" (p. 1332).

In the *Agenda for Lutheran Churches and Congregations, III,5, 1996:* "Have mercy on *her/him* who has fallen asleep in Christ. Receive *her/him* into the communion of the blessed and fulfilled" (no. 23, 174). "We commend *our sister/our brother* into your gracious hand. Have mercy on *her/him* for the sake of Christ and make *her/him* perfect according to your goodness" (no. 28, 179).

[9] DH 1820.

[10] Apol 21:4 (Kolb and Wengert, 238): "Our confession approves giving honor to the saints. This honor is threefold. The first is thanksgiving: we ought to give thanks to God because he has given examples of his mercy . . . The second kind of veneration is the strengthening of our faith . . . The third honor is imitation: first of their faith, then of their other virtues, which people should imitate according to their callings."

[11] CA 21 (Kolb and Wengert, 58f.).

[12] SA II, 2 (Kolb and Wengert, 305).

[13] DH 1821: "The saints, who reign together with Christ, offer up their own prayers to God for men. Thus, it is good and useful *(bonum atque utile)* to invoke them for help, and to have recourse to their prayers, support, and aid for obtaining benefits from God, through His Son, Jesus Christ our Lord, who alone is our Redeemer and Savior."

[14] The complete text of the "Decretum de invocatione, veneratione et reliquis Sanctorum, et sacris imaginibus" is found in *Decrees of the Ecumenical Councils*, Norman Tanner, ed. (London: Sheed & Ward, 1990) vol. 2, 774–76. The excerpts from the Decretal DH 1821–1825 omit this admonition.

[15] CIC can. 1187.

[16] CA 21 (Kolb and Wengert, 58).

[17] SC 8; LG 50ff.

[18] The practice in congregations varies. The Day of St. Michael and All Angels, if it falls on a Sunday, is celebrated; other days (e.g., Peter and Paul) are celebrated in many regions on the basis of tradition; other days only in particularly liturgically oriented congregations (cf. *Evangelisches Gesangbuch* 123:10; 191; 150:4–5).

[19] SC 8; LG chs. V and VII.

[20] Since the Middle Ages the veneration given to Mary, the Mother of God, has been designated as *hyperdulia*. That differs absolutely from the worship of God.

[21] Origen, *On Prayer*, in *An Exhortation to Martyrdom, Prayer, and Selected Works*, translated by Rowan Greer (New York: Paulist Press, 1979) 102.

[22] Apology 21:9 (Kolb and Wengert, 238): "Besides, we also grant that angels pray for us. For there is a passage in Zech 1 [:12] where the angel prays: 'Lord of hosts, how long will you withhold mercy from Jerusalem . . . ?' To be sure, concerning the saints we grant that in heaven they pray for the church in general, just as the saints they prayed for the entire church while living. Nevertheless, there are no testimonies in Scripture about the dead praying, except that of a dream recorded in 2 Maccabees [15:14]."

[23] German: "Evangelische Namenskalender." Jahrbuch für Hymnologie und Liturgik, Bd. 19 (Hannover 1975); cf. also the Evangelischer Kirchenjahrkalender, published each year by the Lutheran Liturgical Conference of Germany [Trans.: Cf. also *The Lutheran Book of Worship* (Minneapolis and Philadelphia 1977) 10–12.]

[24] Augustine, Ep. 78:3, in *Letters 1-99*, Roland Teske, trans. (Hyde Park, N.Y.: New City Press, 2001) 305.

[25] Cf. Thomas à Kempis, *The Imitation of Christ*, I, 23; Leo Sherley-Price, trans. (New York: Penguin, 1952) 58; SA 2:2:18-20 (Kolb and Wengert, 304f.).

[26] LG 68.

[27] *The Creeds:* (Kolb and Wengert, 19–25); the Virginity: CA III (38–39); SA Preface I, II:1 (300); FC Solid Declaration 8 (620); the Mother of God: Apol. 21 (214); FC Ep. 8 (510); SD 8 (620).

[28] Martin Luther, *Luther's Works*, vol. 21 (St. Louis: Concordia Publishing House, 1959) 326.; WA 7:572.

[29] Paul VI, Apostolic Exhortation, *Marialis cultus,* on the veneration of Mary (2.2, 1974), in *The Pope Speaks* 19.1 (1974) 49–87.

[30] *Evangelischer Erwachsenenkatechismus,* 5th ed. (1989) 416.

[31] Vatican II, LG, ch. VIII. On the post-conciliar development, see esp. Paul VI, Apostolic Exhortation *Marialis cultus,* cited above.

[32] Paul VI, Apostolic Exhortation, *Marialis cultus,* pars. 29–39, cited above.

[33] M. Luther, "Sermon for the Festival of the Visitation" (1516) WA 1:60f.

Chapter 8

Steps on the Path to Full Communion

(269) The result of the dialogue on *Communio Sanctorum—the Church as the Communion of Saints* is a contribution to the overall dialogue of our churches on various levels with the goal of reaching full communion. The history of the dialogue shows that the path to this goal is a growth in consensus. This also has been confirmed in the experience of the Bilateral Working Group.

(270) The content of the present text goes beyond previous ecumenical agreements and aims in the process of reception at overcoming reservations and the obstacles that divide us. The results of the Working Group could only be reached by an intensive clarification of our standpoints, by relating the theological statements of the other side to one's own faith, and through the continually confirmed recognition that our common center is in Jesus Christ, who is our salvation and who, in the church, works this salvation for us and the world. Theological discussion and spiritual experience in prayer, worship, and shared struggle for the truth have come together in this dialogue.

(271) A solid basis for agreement in difficult questions was the agreement that Holy Scripture, as "the unsurpassable norm for the church, proclamation, and faith,"[1] is the fundamental and decisive measure for all other witnessing authorities. These authorities—tradition (i.e., the "passing on of the binding apostolic message . . . ."[2]), the faith sense of all the faithful *(sensus fidelium),* the teaching office of the church, and academic theology—are not to be viewed in isolation, but rather must be seen in their relation to Scripture and to each another.

(272)   In the sections on the *Communion of Saints beyond Death*, as well as on the veneration of saints and of Mary, the manner of speaking in which the working group expresses its commonality is of a different type than in the previous chapters. These sections deal in particular with questions about the piety that is embedded within the dynamics of human life. This also has shaped the theological genre and linguistic style of the text. Beyond basic statements that can be agreed upon, specifically Catholic areas of piety are presented with the goal of creating evangelical access to them. It holds here for Catholic understanding that theology takes up evolved contents and forms of piety in order to organize them within the framework of the fundamental and saving truths of revelation and to subordinate them to these truths. Reception might be aided by such a reciprocity, i.e., a path from the reality of lived faith in the Church to the essence of the church and its sending by the Risen Lord in the authority he promised.

(273)   Among the results that point forward is consensus in the description of the common goal: a structured form of unity in which the churches agree in their understanding of the gospel, recognize each other as the church of Jesus Christ, have unreserved communion in the sacraments and mutually recognize their ministerial offices to which word and sacrament are entrusted. Our churches consider themselves committed to this goal, which is oriented toward the communion of world Christianity.[3] They also know that this goal can only be found and reached with the help of the Holy Spirit. The Working Group itself also experienced this help many times during its work, and thanks the Lord for it.

(274)   The convergence reached in this dialogue of the Bilateral Working Group must prove itself in the teaching and practice of our churches. Because it is intended to contribute to a comprehensive mutual understanding and acceptance, reception must proceed on all levels of church teaching and life.

Notes

[1] See above, par. 72.
[2] See above, par. 56; cf. par. 48.
[3] Cf. above, par. 199.